The Gita Story

The Gita Story

Finding answers when life feels hard

Nityanand Charan Das

First Indian Edition,
Published in 2025 by:
Embassy Book Distributors
120, Great Western Building, Maharashtra Chamber of
Commerce Lane, Fort, Mumbai 400 023, India
Tel: (+9122) -30967415, 22819546
Email: info@embassybooks.in
www.embassybooks.in

ISBN: 978-81-19727-68-1

Distribution Centres:
Mumbai, Ahmedabad, Bangalore, Kolkata, Chennai, Hyderabad,
New Delhi, Pune

Cover Design by Rishikumar Thakur for Embassy Book Distributors
Cover & Inside Illustrations by Onkar Fondekar
Printed and bound in India by Thomson Press India Ltd.

Table of Content

Preface

The Gita: A Song Meant for Your Soul

What if I told you that a 5,000-year-old dialogue held the answers to your deepest questions?

What is the purpose of my life?

Why do I struggle within myself?

What happens after death?

How can I stay peaceful in this chaotic world?

How can I connect with the Divine?

This is exactly what the *Bhagavad Gita* does. But it doesn't answer with theory—it answers with a story. A real, raw, soul-awakening conversation between a confused warrior and the God Himself.

This book you now hold is a humble attempt to retell that sacred dialogue in a way that flows like a story—one that's simple, heart-touching, and deeply devotional, yet true to the teachings of the great saints of the past who have shaped countless lives.

This is not a translation. It is not a commentary.

It is an invitation.

An invitation to walk beside Arjuna…

To sit on the chariot…

To look into Krishna's eyes…

And to feel the truth that can guide your life, starting right now.

Why Story Style?

Many readers—especially millennials and youth—yearn for something they can feel, not just study. They want a sacred book that speaks to their heart, not just their intellect.

So, each chapter of the *Gita* has been articulated as a devotional narrative, where Krishna's timeless instructions flow like a river of wisdom through scenes, emotions, and reflections—just as Arjuna experienced them.

Based on Srila Prabhupada's Teachings

This book stands on the shoulders of His Divine Grace A.C. Bhaktivedanta Swami Prabhupada (Founder Acharya of ISKCON), the pure devotee who gifted the *Bhagavad Gita "As It Is"* to the world—now the largest ever sold. Every idea here, every reflection, every lesson, flows from the seed of his original teachings, simplified and reshaped only to resonate with the modern heart.

What You'll Discover

- A clear, flowing retelling of all 18 chapters
- Deep truths wrapped in simple words
- Modern reflections on food, work, stress, happiness, and love
- The path to peace—not through detachment alone, but through devotion
- Krishna—not as a concept, but as a living, loving Presence in your heart

Read with Your Heart

Whether this is your first encounter with the *Gita* or the hundredth time you return to its pages, read slowly. Reflect deeply. Let Krishna speak through these words. And when your heart feels moved, even slightly, know that your real journey has begun.

You don't have to be perfect.

You don't need to understand every Sanskrit term.

You just need to be sincere.

Krishna sees your intention. He always has.

And through the *Gita*, He calls you home.

With folded hands and a grateful heart, I welcome you on this journey.

Hare Krishna.

Nityanand Charan Das

A fellow seeker

Introduction

adhyayanam ca yo nityaṁ

gītāyāḥ satataṁ naraḥ

saṅgrāmeṣu vijayī syāt

trailokyeśv api durlabham

– (Gita Mahatmya)

"One who studies the Gita daily is always victorious—even in the greatest battles. Such victory is rare even among the rulers of the three worlds."

Why the World's Greatest Conversation Still Matters More Than Ever

Once upon a time—on a battlefield, not in a temple—God spoke.

Not in a calm forest. Not in a Himalayan cave. But in the middle of war drums, breaking hearts, and shattered illusions.

That's the *Bhagavad Gita*.

It's not just an ancient scripture. It's a manual for your inner war—the one between fear and faith, confusion and clarity, giving up and standing tall.

But how did it come to this?

The stage was set on the fields of Kurukshetra. Arjuna, a great warrior, stood ready to fight a war he never wanted—with his own relatives, teachers, and friends on the other side. Torn between duty and despair, he dropped his bow. His hands trembled. His heart broke.

In that moment of breakdown, Krishna—his charioteer, friend, and God—spoke.

And what followed was not just advice. It was a divine outpouring of timeless truth—700 verses that would echo through eternity.

Why This Book?

Because you don't need Sanskrit to feel Krishna's message. You don't need a degree in theology to walk Arjuna's path. You just need a heart that's searching.

This book retells the *Bhagavad Gita* as a powerful narrative journey—simple, gripping, and emotionally real. Each chapter is an unfolding scene. Each verse becomes a dialogue that feels like it's happening inside you. Arjuna becomes your voice.

Krishna becomes your guide.

Why Read (and Re-Read) This?

Because life today is still a Kurukshetra.

One moment you're chasing success, the next you're drowning in stress. You want clarity but get confusion. You crave peace but feel pulled in a thousand directions.

That's why Krishna's words still heal.

"This knowledge is the king of education, the most secret of all secrets... It is joyfully performed and everlasting."

- Bhagavad Gita 9.2

"One who studies this sacred conversation worships Me with their intelligence."

- Bhagavad Gita 18.70

Reading the *Gita* isn't about becoming religious. It's about becoming anchored—in who you are, why you're here, and how to walk through life without losing yourself.

What You'll Learn

- How to make decisions without anxiety
- How to do your work without burnout
- How to stay steady when life gets messy
- How to live with purpose, serve with love, and rise above fear
- And most importantly—how to connect with Krishna (God), your eternal well-wisher

One Book. Endless Impact.

This is a story you'll want to revisit often—because each time, it reveals something new. The *Gita* doesn't grow old. You grow deeper.

So, if you're searching for meaning, battling burnout, or simply ready to level up your inner life, start here.

Let Arjuna's questions become yours.

Let Krishna's answers become your compass.

Let this be the story that changes yours.

paṭhyaḥ ślokaḥ priyo nāma
dhyānaṁ tasya sadā śubham
yaḥ smaret pāṭhakaṁ dhīraṁ
sa yāti paramāṁ śivam
– (Gita Mahatmya)

"*Even a single verse of the Gita, when read, remembered, or meditated upon with sincerity, leads the reader to supreme auspiciousness.*"

Main Characters in the *Bhagavad Gita*

Krishna

Krishna is the Supreme Lord and the speaker of the *Bhagavad Gita*. He appears on Earth to guide, protect, and uplift humanity. In the *Gita*, He plays the role of Arjuna's charioteer but also reveals His divine identity as the source of all creation and the ultimate goal of life.

Arjuna

Arjuna is a great warrior and prince, one of the five Pandava brothers. He is known for his skill in archery and his strong sense of dharma (duty). At the start of the battle, he becomes overwhelmed with doubt and grief and turns to Krishna for guidance—this conversation becomes the *Bhagavad Gita*.

The Pandavas

The Pandavas are five righteous brothers—Yudhishthira, Bhima, Arjuna, Nakula, and Sahadeva—born into the Kuru dynasty. They represent virtue, justice, and devotion. They are fighting in the war of Kurukshetra to reclaim their rightful kingdom.

The Kauravas

The Kauravas are the cousins and rivals of the Pandavas, led by the eldest brother Duryodhana. They unlawfully took over the kingdom and refused to return it, which led to the war. The Kauravas represent ambition, envy, and injustice.

Sanjaya

Sanjaya is the charioteer and assistant to King Dhritarashtra. He is given divine vision by the sage Vyasa so, while sitting inside the palace, he narrates the entire battlefield conversation between

Krishna and Arjuna to the blind king. He serves as the narrator of the *Gita*.

Dhritarashtra

Dhritarashtra is the blind king of Hastinapura and the father of the Kauravas. He listens to Sanjaya's narration of the war. Though he knows his sons are wrong, he is emotionally attached to them and unable to stop their actions.

Chapter 1

The Battlefield of the Heart

The Scene is Set—Kurukshetra Awaits!

The dust of war had begun to rise over the sacred land of Kurukshetra—a place not just of battles, but of sacred yajnas (Vedic rituals) and pilgrimage for millions of years. Armies had assembled on both sides, flags fluttered in the wind, conch shells echoed through the sky, and the great Mahabharata war was moments away from unfolding.

Far away from the battlefield, the blind king Dhritarashtra sat in his palace, anxious and restless. Though blind in sight, he was not blind to the gravity of the moment—his sons, the Kauravas, were about to face the Pandavas, the sons of Pandu, in a battle that could change the fate of the world.

Unable to see the war himself, he turned to Sanjaya, his faithful charioteer who had been granted divine vision by the sage Vyasa.

Dhritarashtra asked, “O Sanjaya, in the holy land of Kurukshetra, what did my sons and the sons of Pandu do—after they had gathered, eager to fight?”

Sanjaya, with his eyes now gifted with spiritual sight, gazed inward and began to describe the scene: The warriors were aligned, ready, hearts pounding with valour and pride. On the Kauravas side, the arrogant prince Duryodhana, burning with ambition and fear, noticed the powerful army of the Pandavas arranged strategically.

He quickly approached his teacher, Dronacharya, the master of weapons and warfare who had once trained both the Kauravas and the Pandavas. But today, he stood aligned with the Kauravas, torn by duty and sentiment.

Pointing toward the Pandavas army, Duryodhana sarcastically said, “O my teacher, look at the mighty army of the sons of Pandu—skilfully arranged by your own brilliant disciple Dhrishtadyumna, the son of Drupada.”

He indicated to Drona that his teaching the art of weaponry to Dhrishtadyumna was a big mistake because today he was leading the opposite army.

His voice, though loud, betrayed a tremor of concern. Before them stood warriors of unimaginable strength and legendary skill.

Sanjaya continued narrating to the blind king, painting a scene not just of swords and shields, but of emotions, destinies, and the silent hand of the Divine (Krishna), orchestrating it all.

The Tension Builds

Duryodhana, still speaking to Dronacharya, pointed out the warriors on the Pandavas' side—not with admiration, but with unease wrapped in pride.

"There are great heroes on their side," he declared, "like Bhima and Arjuna, and others equal to them in battle—Yuyudhana, Virata, and the mighty Drupada."

He continued naming them, almost as if counting his fears: Dhrishtaketu, Chekitana, the heroic Kashi Raja, Purujit, Kuntibhoja, and the fearless Shaibya. Each name felt like a drumbeat of destiny.

Then came Yudhamanyu, Uttamauja, and of course, the sons of Subhadra and Draupadi, all noble warriors, all prepared to give everything.

Though Duryodhana tried to appear confident, his eyes flickered. He turned the conversation back to his own side: "But we have heroes too—yourself, Bhishma, Karna, Kripa… powerful, unmatched, ready to lay down their lives for me."

He spoke of Ashwatthama—Drona's own son—Vikarna, and Bhurishrava, warriors fierce and deadly. "Our army," he said, "guarded by Bhishma, is strong… and the Pandavas' army, protected by Bhima, is no match."

Now seeking to rouse his own forces, Duryodhana urged them: "All of you, protect Grandfather Bhishma at all costs! He is the key to our victory."

And Then It Happened

The conch shells began to blow.

Bhishma, the grandsire of the Kuru dynasty, elder to them all, picked up his divine conch and blew it thunderously, his white beard flowing like a mountain breeze. It was like the roar of a lion echoing through the battlefield, charging the Kaurava army with confidence and fire.

The sound awakened the warriors—on both sides. Weapons shimmered, banners waved, and fate moved one step closer to its turning point.

Then came a moment of divine beauty.

From the Pandava side, seated on a majestic chariot drawn by white horses, stood Lord Krishna and Arjuna. The Lord held the reins; the devotee held the bow.

Krishna blew His conch—Panchajanya.

Arjuna blew his—Devadatta.

Bhima, the fierce, blew his conch Paundra, which roared like thunder.

One by one, the Pandava warriors blew their sacred shells, and the sky trembled with the symphony of divine resolve. It was not just a call to battle—it was a spiritual sound, shaking the hearts of the Kauravas, instilling them with fear.

Arjuna's Heart Trembles

As the conch shells echoed across the heavens, announcing the start of the greatest war in history, Arjuna, the mighty Pandava warrior, raised his bow.

Yet before releasing even a single arrow, Arjuna turned to his dear friend and charioteer—Lord Krishna. Something was brewing in his mind.

With deep respect, Arjuna spoke: "O Achyuta (Infallible One), please place my chariot between the two armies. I wish to see those assembled here, those I must fight, and those who have come to support the evil-minded Duryodhana."

Krishna, the Supreme Lord, smiled gently. Though the Lord of all creation, today He played the role of a humble charioteer—for the love of His devotee.

He drove the chariot right into the middle of the battlefield, stopping it in front of Bhishma, Drona, and all the kings and warriors of both sides.

Then He said, "Behold, O Partha, the Kauravas assembled before you."

At that moment, Arjuna scanned the battlefield—not with the eyes of a warrior, but with the eyes of a grandson, a student, a cousin, and a brother.

He saw Bhishma, the grandsire who had loved him as his own. He saw Dronacharya, his guru, the very one who had taught him how to wield the bow he now held.

He saw his uncles, cousins, friends, and even the sons of his own friends.

And suddenly, something changed within him.

A deep sorrow began to rise.

His hands trembled. His bow—Gandiva—slipped from his grip. His skin burned. His mouth dried. His limbs felt weak.

With a heart heavy and voice shaken, Arjuna turned to Krishna: "O Madhusudana (Krishna—the killer of the demon Madhu), how can I fight against Bhishma and Drona, worthy of my worship? I would rather live by begging than slay my teachers and elders, even if they are on the side of injustice."

His words spilled forth—not of cowardice, but of compassion and confusion. He feared the destruction not just of lives, but of dharma, of family traditions, of culture and virtue.

He imagined: What would happen if all the men of the dynasty were slain? Who would preserve sacred values? Wouldn't society crumble? Who would protect the women?

Arjuna's noble heart was torn.

With tears streaming from his eyes, he said in despair: "Govinda, I shall not fight."

And with that, the mighty warrior who had never backed down from battle, sat down on the chariot, overcome with grief, having refused to fight.

Key Lessons for the Modern Seeker

1. Emotional vulnerability is not weakness, it's the beginning of wisdom.

When Arjuna, the greatest warrior, admits his confusion, sorrow, and fear, he shows that acknowledging emotional struggle is not failure—it's the first step toward real strength.

Honour your emotions—they are the doorway to your evolution.

2. Success without purpose feels empty.

Standing on the brink of victory, Arjuna questions the meaning of it all. Winning without righteousness, love, or values would only bring hollow success.

Don't chase goals blindly. Ask yourself: *What am I fighting for?* What am I toiling hard for? Success without meaning is just another kind of loss.

Before chasing success, define your soul's mission.

3. The right guide changes everything.

When Arjuna couldn't trust his own mind anymore, he turned to Krishna—someone who sees beyond immediate emotions to eternal truths.

When you're overwhelmed, seek mentors, wisdom, or divine guidance that reconnects you to your higher self, not just your immediate fears.

Seek voices that lift you higher, not louder.

4. Before every outer battle, there is an inner battle.

Before lifting a weapon, Arjuna had to confront the deeper war within—between attachment and duty, fear and courage, despair and hope.

Your biggest battles aren't outside—they're inside. Mastering your inner world is the key to navigating the outer one.

Win the war within—the outer victories will follow.

5. Real growth begins where comfort ends.

Arjuna wanted to escape, to walk away from a painful duty. But true growth demanded that he stay, reflect, and rise above his immediate emotions.

When life feels uncomfortable or overwhelming, it might not mean you're failing—it could be a part of evolution.

Lean into discomfort; it's the birthplace of your greatness.

Chapter 2

The Essence

The conch shells had quieted. The banners stood still. And in the middle of the sacred battlefield of Kurukshetra, something unexpected had happened.

Arjuna—the mightiest archer of his time, the warrior who had never known defeat—was now trembling. His bow, Gandiva, had slipped from his hands. His voice was choked. Tears streamed from his eyes. Compassion and grief swirled in his heart, paralysing his resolve.

Arjuna's Confusion Continues

He had turned to Lord Krishna, not as a friend or comrade, but as someone desperately seeking answers in the face of an unbearable moral crisis.

It was at this moment that Krishna, seated beside him on the chariot, broke His silence.

His eyes were filled with compassion, yet His voice carried the sharpness of divine clarity.

"My dear Arjuna, from where has this weakness come upon you at this critical moment? This sentimentality is not befitting a warrior, nor one who knows the higher purpose of life. It will lead you only to disgrace and misery."

Arjuna looked at Krishna, stunned. These were not words of comfort—but of awakening.

Krishna leaned closer, His words cutting through Arjuna's fog of doubt.

"O Arjuna, cast off this petty faintheartedness. It does not become you. Abandon this weakness. Stand and fight."

Arjuna swallowed hard. The dilemma in his heart still raged. He tried to explain:

"O Madhusudana, how can I fight those who have been like fathers to me? Bhishma, the grandsire who loved me… Drona, my revered teacher… How can I raise my bow against them? I would rather live by begging than win a kingdom soaked in the blood of those I honour."

He paused, his strength fading like a flame in the wind.

"Even if they are on the wrong side of wrong, still… I cannot bear the thought of killing them. My heart is breaking, Krishna."

And then—something sacred happened.

Arjuna's proud shoulders lowered. His voice softened. Realising he could not overcome his deep emotional turmoil on his own, his eyes met Krishna's with humility and spoke:

"I do not know what is right anymore. I am confused. My mind is overwhelmed. I surrender to You, Krishna. You are my guide now, my spiritual master (Guru) and I am your disciple. Please instruct me. Tell me what is truly best for me."

That surrender was not weakness—it was the beginning of transformation.

Arjuna, once the undefeatable warrior, had now become a disciple. And Krishna, the Supreme Lord of all creation, was ready to reveal the eternal wisdom of the *Gita*.

Sanjaya, the mystic seer narrating this sacred moment to King Dhritarashtra, described what happened next: "Thus, Arjuna, surrounded by enemies yet paralysed by compassion, laid down his bow and sat down on the chariot—his heart heavy with sorrow."

But this was not the end of Arjuna's journey. In truth, it was the beginning.

The battlefield of Kurukshetra was now a sacred classroom.

And Lord Krishna—Jagadguru, the universal teacher—was about to speak words that would illuminate not just Arjuna's heart, but the hearts of seekers for millennia to come.

The Wisdom of the Soul

Arjuna sat still on the chariot, his bow resting on the floor, his heart burdened by grief and confusion. The battlefield faded in his mind, and all that remained was the sound of Krishna's voice—clear, calm, and filled with transcendental wisdom.

Krishna looked at Arjuna with deep affection. Now was the time to speak—not merely as a friend, but as the eternal guide of all living beings.

"You are grieving for those who are not worthy of grief, Arjuna. Wise men do not lament for the living or the dead."

Arjuna looked up—startled. These words were unexpected. How could grief for loved ones not be justified?

But Krishna continued, unveiling a truth that lies beyond life and death: "We are not our bodies. We are the souls, spiritual beings, within the bodies... Never was there a time when I did not exist, nor you, nor all these kings. And never shall we cease to exist in the future."

"Just as the embodied soul passes through childhood, youth, and old age in this life, in the same way, it passes on to another body after death. The wise are not bewildered by this change. Death is just another change for the better."

Arjuna listened—his mind beginning to stir from the slumber of illusion.

Krishna's voice was now gentle, but resolute: "The pleasure and pain in this world are like changing of seasons. These experiences come and go. They are temporary, O Arjuna. Endure them with courage. Nothing is permanent."

And then came one of the most profound statements of the *Gita*—a verse that echoes eternally in the hearts of seekers: "That which is real (the soul) never ceases to be. That which is unreal (the body) never truly stays. The truth has been seen by those who have seen with wisdom."

Krishna revealed the greatest secret of all: "The soul—the atma—cannot be cut by weapons, nor burned by fire, nor wet by water, nor withered by wind. It is eternal, unborn, and unchanging."

"The soul does not kill, nor can it be killed. As one discards old garments and takes on new ones, so the soul discards old bodies and takes new ones."

For a moment, the weight in Arjuna's heart began to lift. The battlefield around him no longer appeared as a scene of impending death, but a stage for duty, transformation, and divine purpose.

Krishna concluded: "Therefore, arise, O Arjuna. Perform your duty. Do not lament. The body will perish one day, no matter how much we try to hold on to it. The soul is eternal, and nothing can harm its real essence, the real 'You'."

In that sacred moment, Krishna wasn't just speaking to Arjuna. He was speaking to all of us—to every soul who has ever felt fear, sorrow, or confusion. He was reminding us that beneath the temporary coverings of the body and mind, we are eternal, spiritual beings—unchanging, unbreakable, and beloved by God.

And this was just the beginning.

Acting Without Attachment

As the weight of Arjuna's sorrow began to lift, Krishna gently shifted the conversation—from the eternity of the soul to the purpose of action in this world.

His words now carried the calm strength of a loving teacher, guiding His disciple through the fog of doubt: "Arjuna, you have a right to perform your prescribed duty, but you are not entitled to the results of your actions. Never be attached to the fruits of work, and never shirk your duty either."

That single teaching struck like lightning in Arjuna's heart.

Act, but do not get affected by the results (because they are dependent on many factors and not just our efforts).

Do your duty, but don't claim ownership. The only thing within our control is our effort. The more we focus on what we can control, the more we become free from anxiety.

Krishna continued: "O Arjuna. Perform your actions with an even mind. Success or failure—treat them the same. This equanimity is called yoga (union with God's will)."

Arjuna's world had been governed by outcomes: victory and defeat, gain and loss. But now Krishna was showing him a higher path—where one acts not for reward, but as an offering, a duty, a service, a sacred expression of devotion to God.

"Such work done without attachment, with a steady mind, delivers one from bondage of karma and brings peace."

Arjuna's gaze began to shift—not outward to the battlefield, but inward, toward clarity.

Krishna continued to peel back the layers of illusion: "O Dhananjaya, give up all desires born of the ego. Anchor your mind in the soul. Be undisturbed by gain or loss, and you shall live in the state of divine consciousness."

Then Krishna offered the contrast: "Men of small knowledge are attached to flowery words of the Vedas that promise material enjoyment. But you—rise above this. Don't get lost in the rituals meant for mere rewards. Fix your mind on Me, and perform your duty with devotion."

Arjuna sat silently, absorbing each word. His doubts hadn't vanished entirely, but a new light had entered his heart.

Krishna's voice grew soft, and He concluded with a call to rise: "So now, stand up, O Arjuna. With a sword of knowledge, cut through the doubts in your heart. Arise and fight—not for victory or defeat, but for Me."

At that moment, Arjuna wasn't just being prepared for battle.

He was being awakened to a life of transcendental action—a life where work becomes worship, where duty is done without ego, and where success lies not in the outcome, but in doing our best as an offering to the Lord.

This is karma yoga.

This is devotion in motion.

Symptoms of a Divine Mindset

As Krishna spoke about working without attachment, something within Arjuna began to shift. The fog of confusion was slowly clearing. But his heart still had questions—deeper questions.

With folded hands, he turned to his Lord once more.

"O Krishna," he asked, "what are the symptoms of one who is steady in wisdom or the one in divine consciousness? How does such a person speak, sit, or walk? What does it mean to be truly self-realised?"

Krishna's eyes sparkled. This was not just the question of a warrior—it was the question of a seeker.

And so, He answered with compassion and clarity: "One who is undisturbed by desires, who is not shaken by pleasure or pain, and who is satisfied in the self alone—such a person is truly steady in transcendental knowledge."

Such a soul, Krishna said, no longer craves external validation nor is thrown off balance by the highs and lows of life. Due to their spiritual depth, they are like the ocean—vast, deep, and undisturbed—even as rivers of desire flow into them.

"A person who is not agitated by lust, greed, or anger, who is free from attachment and ego, who remains equipoised in all situations—that soul is truly peaceful."

Krishna went on: "Just as a tortoise withdraws its limbs into its shell, the self-realised soul withdraws his senses from sense objects. This detachment is not repression—it is freedom."

But He warned Arjuna: merely withdrawing the senses is not enough. The mind may still carry taste for enjoyment. Only one who has experienced a higher taste—spiritual bliss—can truly overcome lower desires.

The Fall

Then, Krishna described what happens when one falls from the path of self-control: "From attachment, desire is born. From desire, anger arises. Anger leads to delusion; delusion causes forgetfulness of duty. From forgetfulness comes loss of intelligence—and when intelligence is lost, one falls into ruin."

A moment of silence passed as Arjuna absorbed the chain reaction—the subtle fall from desire to destruction.

Krishna continued, pointing to the solution: "But one who controls the mind and engages the senses in My service, who follows the path of devotion with a pure heart—that person remains undisturbed and peaceful."

Such souls live in the light of divine knowledge. Not lured by temporary attractions, not repelled by discomfort—they walk the world untouched, living in it but not of it.

Krishna then ended this chapter with a powerful vision: "That is the state of samādhi—pure, unwavering consciousness. One who attains it is no longer bewildered. Even at the time of death, such a soul remains steady and enters My eternal kingdom."

The sun may have still hung over the Kurukshetra sky, but for Arjuna, a new dawn had already begun—the dawn of inner clarity.

KEY LESSONS FOR THE MODERN SEEKER

1. True wisdom means knowing what we don't know.

The journey begins when we admit, "I don't have all the answers." Arjuna's real transformation didn't start with his strength—it started when he said, "I am confused. I surrender. Please guide me."

Admitting we're lost is the first step to true growth.

2. Feel your emotions, but act wisely.

Krishna didn't shame Arjuna for feeling pain. He reminded him not to let emotion blur his vision of what's right.

Feel deeply, but don't let emotions paralyse your purpose. Move with your values.

3. You are not your wins or losses.

You are not your résumé. You are an eternal, divine soul: a spiritual being. Your essence is sacred and unchanging.

Don't tie your worth to likes, salaries, trophies, or setbacks.

4. Let go of outcomes, hold on to your peace.

Work hard. Love deeply and do your best. But don't chain your happiness to outcomes.

5. Real peace comes from finding a higher taste.

Replace lower pleasures with higher purpose.

We can't just say "no" to temptation—we need a bigger, better "yes". Chase purpose over pleasure. Seek experiences that feed your soul, not just your senses.

True freedom comes when we discover something sweeter than fleeting pleasures—spiritual connection.

Chapter 3

The Sacred Art of Action

The battlefield still roared in the distance, but in Arjuna's heart, the storm had only just begun. After hearing Krishna's profound truths about the soul and self-realisation, Arjuna's mind was still clouded. There was one question that wouldn't leave him.

He turned to Krishna, puzzled and sincere.

"Krishna," he said, "If intelligence is greater than action, and self-realisation is the goal, then why do You urge me to act to fight? Isn't renunciation better?"

Krishna smiled gently. The time had come to address a deep misconception—not just in Arjuna's heart, but in the hearts of countless seekers to come.

"O Arjuna, I've explained two paths: the path of knowledge and the path of selfless action. But simply renouncing work doesn't free one from reaction, nor does idleness lead to perfection. Every soul is forced to act by his/her nature—even against their will."

In that moment, Krishna revealed a timeless truth:

"You can't stop acting—but you can stop being attached."

"One who outwardly restrains the body but dwells on desires in the mind is a pretender. But one who controls the senses and engages in duty with devotion—he is far superior."

Arjuna was beginning to understand. Renunciation was not a matter of leaving the world—it was about purifying your intention in the world. It was about working with the right intention.

Krishna continued: "Perform your prescribed duties, Arjuna. Action is better than inaction. Even maintaining your body requires work. But when actions are done as offerings to Me, they become purifying and free the person from reactions to karma."

And then, Krishna traced the cosmic cycle that keeps the world in harmony: "In the beginning, I created Vedic rituals along with humanity. Through rituals, the celestial gods are pleased. In turn, they provide the necessities of life such as water, heat, light and vegetation. Thus, all prosper together through this system of gratitude towards each other."

"But those who enjoy these gifts without offering them back—they're nothing but thieves," Krishna declared.

He explained that the devotees, those who eat only after offering their food to God, are freed from sin. But those who eat only for themselves—consume only karma.

"O Arjuna, work done in devotion, without attachment, purifies the heart and leads one to Me."

(Examples: 1. No one is forbidden from eating. But before eating, offer the food to Krishna. Thus, it becomes a karma-free diet.

2. No one is forbidden from earning money. But use a portion of it to serve Krishna. One could make a small temple at home, install deities of Radha Krishna or Laxmi Narayan or Sita Ram [as per one's attraction] and worship Krishna with family, hold spiritual gatherings, serve prasad [food offered to God] to the attendees and even use one's wealth and resources to help devotees expand God-consciousness in society.

3. No one is barred from living in a palatial home. But live with the consciousness that it is actually God's home and His mercy.

In essence, make Krishna a loving family member and serve Him as you would any other respectable family member of yours. This way, all our work becomes worship.)

Then Krishna shared the example of the ancient kings who were not just great rulers but great devotees as well: "Even great souls like Janaka performed their duties to set an example. Whatever action a great person does, the rest of the world follows. Arjuna, if I Myself didn't perform duties, the world would fall into ruin."

Arjuna now looked up, captivated.

Krishna leaned in, his words glowing with divine power: "Therefore, perform your duty for My sake, without selfish motives. Fight—not out of hate or pride, but out of service to Me."

He then revealed a subtle danger: "Don't confuse and try to stop those who are attached to results. Instead, lead by example. Guide them slowly. Don't disrupt their minds, but inspire them with your behaviour in how to make spiritual advancement while living a worldly life."

Krishna further said: "You think you're the one doing everything, but really, it's nature that moves the body. Your true self—the soul—is just the witness."

"Those who understand this live freely. They work without pride and stay peaceful. But when you think, 'I am the doer,' ego takes over—and that leads to stress, greed, and pain."

Krishna then offered Arjuna a lifeline: "Therefore, surrender all your works to Me. With full knowledge of Me, free from expectations and possessiveness, fight. You will not be bound by karma."

And then, a warning: "Those who follow this path with faith, free from envy, become liberated. But those who reject it, proud and deluded, are doomed to remain in bondage and suffer."

As Arjuna absorbed these divine truths, Krishna made one

final, stirring revelation: "It's better to fail at being your true self than succeed by copying someone else [because Arjuna wanted to become a sannyasi to avoid the war]. Trying to live another person's life is risky. Do not compare yourself to others—follow your own nature and live your life in alignment with the will of the Supreme Lord."

Arjuna, still wrestling with doubt, asked: "Krishna, why do we sometimes act sinfully—even unwillingly, as if forced?"

Krishna's voice was firm: "It is deep-rooted desire for selfish enjoyment—born of passion—that drives one to sin. Like fire, it devours wisdom. It is your greatest enemy."

"Conquer this enemy, Arjuna. It hides in the senses, mind, and intelligence. But by controlling the senses, and engaging in devotional service by chanting my names and hearing about my activities, you can defeat it."

He ended with a powerful instruction: "Establish yourself in spiritual intelligence. Strengthen your mind. Grow in spiritual wisdom. Calm your cravings. Rise as the peaceful master of your own destiny."

The Chapter Ends, But the War Within Begins

And so, Krishna's call to action was not just a call to arms, but a call to awaken the soul.

He taught Arjuna—and all of us—that spiritual life doesn't mean inactivity or running away from duties. It means offering all that we do to the Supreme, acting as per His will to please Him, without pride, without fear, without attachment.

This is karma yoga—the sacred art of action, purified by love and guided by devotion.

Key Lessons for the Modern Seeker

1. Action is inevitable—attachment is optional.

We can't avoid action in life, but we can avoid attachment to the outcomes. Engage in what you do with devotion and purity of intention, not for personal gain.

2. Live your truth.

Follow your own path, your own calling, to connect with God and stay true to your unique contribution to society by being a good example of how one can make spiritual advancement while executing one's worldly duties.

It is a life of connection, not rejection.

3. Renunciation is not inaction.

Renunciation isn't about quitting the world; it's about purifying our mind and actions. Offering our work to a higher purpose brings spiritual growth.

4. Desire is the real enemy.

Desire, especially when unchecked, is the root cause of suffering and sin. Overcome your desires by focusing on spiritual wisdom and self-control.

5. Work as service.

Offer everything to the Divine—and walk free of karma. Perform your duties selflessly, without pride or ego. When actions are done as an offering to the divine, they become purifying and elevate the soul.

Chapter 4

The Eternal Thread—Krishna Reveals His Divine Secret

The winds over Kurukshetra had stalled, as if the earth itself paused to hear what would be said next.

Arjuna stood facing Krishna—his mind a churning sea of questions, yet his heart finally ready to receive. The battlefield around them remained frozen in anticipation, chariots unmoving, warriors quiet. In this sacred pause, time itself became the student.

Krishna, the charioteer who was also the Master of all universes, began to speak—not as a commander, but as the Eternal Teacher.

"Arjuna, this knowledge I'm sharing with you is not new. It is timeless."

His voice was steady and soft, but every word carried the weight of centuries.

"Long ago, I taught this eternal science (*Bhagavad Gita*) of self-realisation—yoga—to the sun-god Vivasvan. He passed it to Manu, the father of mankind. Manu gave it to Ikshvaku, the great earthly king. Thus, passed from master to disciple, this wisdom guided generations of saintly kings."

Krishna paused, letting the history sink in.

"But over time, Arjuna, this sacred chain was broken. The knowledge became lost to the world. And now—because you are My dear friend and My devotee—I am reviving it once again, through you."

Arjuna blinked, uncertain. His heart trusted Krishna, but his intellect hesitated.

"Krishna… You were born just a few decades ago. The sun-god? Manu? They existed ages ago. How could You have taught them?"

Krishna smiled.

"Ah, My dear Arjuna," He said gently, "You and I have both had many births. I remember all of them—you do not."

And then, like a curtain being drawn back on eternity, Krishna revealed a truth only the Lord can speak:

"Although I am unborn, although My transcendental form never deteriorates, I appear in this world by My own will."

"When righteousness fades and unrighteousness rises, I descend.

Again and again, I come—to protect My devotees, destroy evil, and reestablish dharma."

Arjuna's eyes widened. He wasn't just hearing philosophy—he was standing before that very great personality.

"Whoever understands the divine nature of My birth and activities," Krishna said, "will not be born again. Such a soul, freed from illusion, comes to Me."

A gust of wind swept across the chariot, stirring Arjuna's hair. But his mind had grown still, focused, alert.

Krishna continued: "Many souls in the past, taking shelter in Me—free from desire, fear, and anger—have purified themselves through knowledge and devotion. They have all reached Me. You can too."

And then Krishna spoke a verse that echoed across all walks of life, in every age: "As all surrender unto Me, I reward them accordingly. Everyone follows My path in all respects, O Arjuna."

A hush settled over the space between them.

"Some people chase quick results by worshipping different gods. Some do rituals. But in the end, everything offered reaches Me—I'm the one behind it all."

(Even if people offer worship to different gods or do rituals for quick results, Krishna is the one who ultimately empowers everything—like the CEO behind every department.

But just because the offerings reach Krishna in an indirect way doesn't mean all worship is the same as worshipping Krishna directly. Worshipping the celestial gods is like talking to the assistants; worshipping Krishna is going straight to the Boss Himself.)

"Those who don't know Me think I'm just another being. But the wise, who get who I really am, love and worship Me from the heart."

"I created the system of different roles of individuals (Varnashrama dharma) in society, based on people's talents and actions—not by birth. But I stay beyond it all. I'm not tied down by anything. And if you understand this, you can also live free."

Krishna's gaze deepened.

"Arjuna, intelligent men in the past acted with this understanding. So you, too, should perform your duty—as did they—without attachment."

But now, Krishna shifted tones. His words turned mysterious, as He touched on a subtle truth: "It is a fact that even the wise are bewildered when trying to discern what is action (karma) and what is inaction (akarma). Let Me explain."

"A person who sees inaction in action and action in inaction is truly intelligent. Though acting, he is not entangled."

Arjuna listened with a quiet reverence.

“He whose every act is an offering to the Lord, who seeks no reward, who is content and detached—he becomes free. Just as fire turns wood to ash, the fire of knowledge burns all karma to nothing.”

Then Krishna gave the key: “But how do you receive this knowledge?”

His answer was crystal clear: “Approach a spiritual master. Inquire humbly. Serve him. The self-realised soul can give you this knowledge, for he has seen the truth.”

“And when you gain this knowledge, Arjuna, your doubts will be destroyed. You will see all beings as equal—whether saint or sinner—and you will not be bewildered again.”

A silence passed between them, as if the sky itself waited for the next words.

And then Krishna, the Lord of hearts, gave His final encouragement for this chapter: “Even the greatest sinner, if properly situated in knowledge, can cross over the ocean of suffering. There is no purifier greater than this knowledge. In time, one devoted to Me will attain it naturally.”

“But those without faith—who doubt and disregard the path—they are lost. The doubting soul finds peace neither in this world nor the next.”

And finally: “Therefore, Arjuna, armed with the sword of

knowledge, cut through the doubts in your heart. While staying connected to Me by executing My will, stand and fight (do your duty)."

In That Moment…

The sword of knowledge was drawn. The battlefield of Kurukshetra stood unchanged. But within Arjuna, something had shifted forever.

This was no longer just a conversation about war. It was about identity, eternity, and love.

Krishna had not just spoken about truth—He had revealed Himself as the eternal teacher, the Supreme Lord, the friend who returns age after age… for the sake of one sincere devotee.

And now, Arjuna was no longer alone in the chariot—he was carried by the voice of the Absolute.

KEY LESSONS FOR THE MODERN SEEKER

1. Truth is timeless.

The *Gita's* wisdom isn't new—it's eternal, passed down through generations but often forgotten. Rediscover it.

2. Krishna is beyond time.

He's not just a historical figure—He's the eternal Source behind everything, beyond birth and death.

3. Go straight to the source.

All worship reaches Krishna as He is the source of everyone's powers to grant results, but direct devotion to Him is the fastest and purest path.

4. Act without attachment.

Do your best, but let go of outcomes. True freedom comes when you work for love, not rewards.

5. Kill doubt with knowledge.

Doubt holds you back. Find a genuine guide, seek wisdom, and move forward with faith and clarity.

Chapter 5

The Peace Beyond the Sword—Harmony of Renunciation and Action

As the sacred chariot stood firm on the plains of Kurukshetra, the sun now higher in the sky, Arjuna remained immersed in Krishna's voice—each word a stream of nectar cutting through his confusion.

He had heard of karma yoga—selfless action in devotion. And he had also heard about renunciation—letting go of worldly duty. Both seemed noble. Both seemed powerful. But a question lingered in his heart.

With a respectful glance at his Lord, Arjuna asked: "Krishna, You speak of renunciation of action, and also of action in devotion.

Please tell me clearly—which of the two is better?"

Krishna's face softened, like a teacher smiling at a diligent student.

"Both lead to liberation," He said. "But of the two, karma yoga—action performed in devotional consciousness—is superior."

"One who neither hates nor craves the fruits of action, who performs duties without attachment—that person is truly a renunciate. Such a soul is untouched by reactions, just as a lotus is untouched by the water around it."

And then, the Supreme Lord unveiled a beautiful truth: "True renunciation is not about abandoning work, but about abandoning attachment."

"The wise see no difference between renunciation and devotional action. For the one who sees rightly, both paths lead to the same destination."

Krishna's voice now grew more intimate, more personal.

"But it is easier, Arjuna, to reach perfection through karma yoga, because it keeps the mind engaged while purifying the heart."

"But who is a karma yogi?" a question appeared in Arjuna's mind.

Krishna, sensing it, replied: "A true yogi is one who is free from ego, whose mind is steady, who works for the pleasure of the Lord and not for his own gain. He is not bound by karma."

"He who sees all beings equally—in joy and sorrow, in success and failure—that person is always connected to Me, even while acting in the world."

Arjuna listened in awe. Here was the art of living in the world yet not being of the world.

"Such a soul," Krishna continued, "whose mind is fixed in Me, who is free from material desires and dualities, finds peace."

"He neither rejoices in gain nor laments in loss. His intelligence is steady. He sees the Supreme in all beings, and all beings in the Supreme."

"For him, a learned sage, a cow, an elephant, a dog, and even an outcaste—all are equal."

Arjuna's heart began to stir. This was not just about fighting. This was about freedom—a freedom untouched by weapons or enemies. A freedom from the turmoil within.

Krishna now gently lifted the veil even further: "The material world is full of dualities—pleasure and pain, honour and dishonour. But the yogi who tolerates them, who is not shaken, who remains centred—such a person achieves lasting peace."

"Happiness that comes from contact with the senses is fleeting. It has a beginning and an end. But the yogi, detached from such pleasures, finds a joy that is eternal—within the self."

And then Krishna described this inner joy in exquisite detail: "He who is able to tolerate the urges of lust and anger before death is a yogi and is truly happy."

"Such a liberated soul, always engaged in the welfare of all beings, attains peace. Freed from desire, ego, and possessiveness, he finds Me—his eternal refuge."

"He who sees Me in everything, and everything in Me, is never lost to Me. Nor am I ever lost to him."

By now, Arjuna's eyes were filled with wonder. The war outside had not begun—but the inner war was already being won.

Krishna's final words of this chapter poured forth like a river flowing into the ocean of peace: "The yogi who unites with Me through meditation on my beautiful form and sound of my blessed name (Hare Krishna Hare Krishna, Krishna Krishna Hare Hare, Hare Ram Hare Ram, Ram Ram Hare Hare), who remains detached and pure, who conquers the mind and the senses—he attains My supreme abode."

"This is the path of peace, Arjuna—not by rejection of the world, but by seeing Me within it all."

In That Moment…

The battle of the mind began to settle.

As the wind danced through the fields of Kurukshetra, Arjuna stood not as a man torn between action and inaction, but as a soul beginning to see the middle path.

Not to run from the world.

Not to cling to it.

But to serve within it, with a heart offered to Krishna.

Renunciation wasn't escape. It was transformation.

And action, when done in devotion, became liberation.

Krishna had not just answered Arjuna's question—He had harmonised the two great rivers of spirituality: wisdom and work.

And now, the stage was set for the deeper meditation that would follow…

Key Lessons for the Modern Seeker

1. Don't quit the world—purify your role in it.

You don't need to be a monk to be spiritual. Live your purpose, but let go of the need for control and validation. Do your best, offer the rest.

2. Peace is found in inner balance, not outer success.

Stop chasing likes, promotions, or perfect outcomes. Lasting peace comes when you're anchored inside—not tossed around by the world.

3. Equality is the vision of a liberated soul.

True spirituality isn't just about rituals—it's how you treat people. Respect all beings, regardless of status, gender, race, or background.

4. The middle path is the strongest one.

You don't have to renounce life. Just shift why you act. Serve with love keeping the Lord's satisfaction in mind. Let go of the results. That's yoga in action.

5. Real joy doesn't depend on the senses.

Dopamine fades, but devotion stays. Trade binge-scrolling for soul-scrolling. Dive into mantra (Hare Krishna Hare Krishna, Krishna Krishna Hare Hare, Hare Ram Hare Ram, Ram Ram Hare Hare), meaning, and meditation—it's where real happiness begins.

Chapter 6

The Silent Warrior—Yoga of Meditation

The dust of Kurukshetra still lingered in the air, but Arjuna's heart was no longer burdened by fear. Something inside him had begun to awaken—not just as a warrior, but as a seeker.

He had heard Krishna speak of selfless action, renunciation, and the art of living in devotion. But now, Arjuna longed to understand something deeper:

What happens when one turns completely inward? When the battle is not just outside, but within?

Sensing this, Krishna began to reveal another path—not of weapons, nor politics, but of silence, discipline, and stillness.

"He is a true renunciate and yogi (connected to God)," Krishna said, "who performs his duty without attachment to results—not one who merely gives up all work or external rituals."

Arjuna blinked. That was unexpected.

Krishna continued, calm as the Ganga flowing through the Himalayas: "Renunciation and yoga are one. Unless a person gives up the desire for personal gain, he cannot be a true yogi."

Then, like a master archer revealing the hidden target, Krishna pointed inward: "When a person has conquered the mind and senses, when he is satisfied in the Self alone—he is said to be truly situated in yoga (connection with God)."

He painted a picture with words: "Such a soul is unshaken by heat or cold, honour or dishonour, joy or sorrow. He remains equal to all and is firmly fixed in transcendence."

"He neither clings to people nor avoids them. He is content, self-controlled, and always absorbed in the Supreme. This is the true yogi."

Arjuna now listened, spellbound. Each word felt like a thread being woven into a sacred fabric.

Then Krishna spoke of the discipline of meditation—what the world would later call dhyana yoga: "Let the yogi go to a secluded place. Let him sit on a seat that is neither too high nor too low, made of kusa grass, a deerskin, and cloth. There, with a mind focused and senses restrained, let him practise self-realisation."

"With the back straight, the gaze steady, and the mind fixed on Me alone, he should meditate—not thinking of anything else."

"And how should he live?" Krishna asked, as if reading Arjuna's thoughts.

"Not too much eating, not too little. Not excessive sleep, not wakefulness. Balanced in habits of work, rest, and recreation—that person becomes free from all sorrows."

Krishna now revealed the fruit of such meditation: "When the mind, disciplined by yoga, becomes steady like a lamp in a windless place, then one is said to be in samadhi—deep spiritual absorption where the mind does not waver from the Lord even for a moment."

"In that state, one experiences unending spiritual joy—realised through the purified heart. That happiness is beyond the senses, yet it satisfies the soul."

"And once having tasted it, one never returns to worldly pleasures, for he has found the treasure of the Self."

Arjuna's eyes were wide, yet peaceful. This was no fantasy—this was the deep inner life of the saintly yogi.

But Krishna wasn't done yet.

"This yoga must be practised with determination and faith. The yogi must guard against distraction, keeping the mind always fixed on Me."

"Wherever the mind wanders, bring it back under the control of the Self. The yogi whose mind is thus disciplined finds peace."

And then Krishna revealed something even more intimate: "Of all yogis, the one who worships Me with devotion, thinking of Me always, is the most intimately united with Me."

"He is the highest of all."

Arjuna's Question: What if One Fails?

Moved by the lofty path, Arjuna asked a heartfelt question—one that echoes in the hearts of spiritual seekers even today: "Krishna, what happens to the person who begins his spiritual journey towards you but fails to attain perfection? Does he perish like a cloud scattered by the wind?"

Krishna, ever the compassionate guide, reassured him: "No, Arjuna. A transcendentalist never meets destruction—either in this life or the next."

"Such a soul is reborn in a righteous, aristocratic family—or even in a family of great souls. There, he resumes his journey from where he left off."

"And with sincere effort, he will naturally be drawn toward the Supreme, as if by memory from a previous life."

"Eventually, through many births of practice, he achieves perfection and reaches Me."

Krishna's voice now grew warm and tender: "The yogi is greater than the ascetic. Greater than the scholar. Greater than the ritualistic performer. Therefore, Arjuna, become a yogi (always stay connected to me)."

"And of all yogis, one who worships Me with full faith and devotion, who offers his heart to Me—he is most dear to Me."

In That Moment...

Krishna concluded this sacred chapter—not with a rule, but with a revelation of love.

The journey inward was not about escaping the world, but about discovering the Self within—and surrendering that Self to the Supreme.

A yogi was not just a man sitting in a forest. A yogi was anyone who saw Krishna everywhere, and who offered his thoughts, words, and actions back to Him.

That was the perfection of meditation.

That was the height of yoga.

That was the heart of bhakti.

And for Arjuna—for all of us—it was a path not just to peace, but to eternal connection with the Lord of our hearts.

Key Lessons for the Modern Seeker

1. Stillness is strength.

In a world addicted to noise and hustle, stillness isn't weakness—it's mastery. Real warriors don't just conquer the world; they conquer their own restless minds. Meditation is your daily training ground.

2. Balance over burnout.

The *Gita* isn't asking you to run away to the mountains. It's asking you to find balance—between work and rest, ambition and contentment, solitude and connection. Balance is the new success.

3. Don't fear failure—spiritual progress is never lost.

Started your devotional journey but stopped? Tried spirituality but got distracted? Krishna says: it's okay. Every sincere effort counts. Even one step towards truth is carried over. You're never starting from scratch.

4. Discipline the mind, find inner peace.

Your mind is like a puppy—it will wander. Don't scold it; train it. With practice, you'll learn to pause, breathe, and redirect your thoughts toward Krishna. This is yoga, off the mat.

5. The highest yogi loves deeply.

Yoga isn't just posture or silence—it's love. The one who lives with devotion, who remembers the Divine with sincerity, even in the chaos of life, is the true yogi. Love is the shortcut to liberation.

Chapter 7

The Hidden Presence

The battlefield of Kurukshetra lay hushed. The conch shells had echoed. Warriors stood poised. Yet within Arjuna's heart, a new battle stirred—one not of arrows or armies, but of understanding.

He had already surrendered. He was no longer merely a prince or a hero—he was now a seeker, a disciple.

And Krishna—his charioteer, friend, and now revealed as the Supreme Lord—continued to reveal the layers of truth, each one deeper than the last.

Now, the Lord's voice shifted again. It carried the resonance of eternity, as if the entire cosmos had paused to listen.

"Arjuna," He said gently, "listen now as I reveal knowledge that is both theoretical (jñāna) and realised (vijñāna). This wisdom is the crown jewel, the essence of all truth. Once you know this, nothing further will remain to be known."

Arjuna's breath caught. Was such a thing even possible—to know everything simply by knowing Krishna?

Krishna nodded slowly. "Yet out of thousands, few strive for perfection. And of those, very few truly understand Me as I am."

The humility of that truth struck deep. Not just devotion, but pure understanding of Krishna was rare—because Krishna was not just a god among gods. He was the origin, the source, the heart of all that is.

And then Krishna did something profound. He lifted the veil of nature itself.

"Arjuna," He said, "this world is made of My separated energies—earth, water, fire, air, ether… mind, intelligence, and ego. These form the material nature that surrounds you."

"But beyond all this," He continued, "is My higher energy—the living beings themselves. The souls who animate this world, who think, strive, and live… they are My own."

Arjuna blinked. We are part of You?

"Yes," Krishna said, reading his thoughts. "All living beings are My energy. Everything moves by My power, though I remain unseen—just like a thread holds pearls together, I bind the universe."

Krishna's eyes softened, and His words grew intimate: "I am the taste of water, Arjuna. The light of the sun and moon. The syllable Om in the Vedas. The sound in space. The ability in man."

Arjuna's heart trembled. The divine was no longer distant. Krishna was revealing Himself to be everywhere—in the fragrance of earth, the fire of digestion, the intelligence of the wise, the strength that is free from pride.

But then came the sorrowful truth.

"People do not know Me," Krishna said. "They are bewildered by My divine energy, Māyā. Though I am unborn and eternal, they think I have taken this human form like them. This illusion covers their eyes."

Arjuna's heart ached. How many chase temporary pleasures, not knowing they're chasing shadows?

"Indeed," Krishna said, "four kinds of people, if they are fortunate, turn towards Me: those in distress, the curious, the seeker of wealth, and the truly wise. Of them, the wise one—who worships Me with love, knowing Me as the cause of all—is most dear to Me. And I am dear to him."

But Krishna did not withhold the darker side of truth. With sober gravity, He added: "There are also four types who never surrender to Me—those who are foolish, those who are too proud and consider themselves all-knowing, those whose knowledge is stolen by illusion, and those who are overtly demonic in nature. Their hearts are closed by envy and arrogance, and thus they are deprived of the grace that opens the path to Me."

It was a sobering reminder. The path to Krishna was open to all—but not all wished to walk it.

For a moment, the battlefield vanished. In its place stood a deeper truth—that Krishna was not just the commander of cosmic forces, but a loving Lord, eager to be loved in return.

"But even such a wise soul," Krishna added, "takes many births to reach Me. After lifetimes of sincere search, one finally understands and declares: Vāsudevah sarvam iti—Krishna is everything."

Krishna's voice now carried both strength and compassion: "Many are misled by desires. They worship other deities, seeking quick rewards. And I grant those rewards, for it is I alone who fulfil their faith. But the results are temporary. Those who worship heavenly gods go to those gods. Those who worship Me come to Me."

Arjuna looked up, tears brimming in his eyes. Why is it so hard to recognise You, my Lord?

Krishna answered: "Because I do not reveal Myself to everyone. I am covered by My own spiritual energy, and only those who are free from selfish desires, who are engaged in My devotional service, can truly know Me."

And then, with divine gravity, Krishna spoke the truth that

would echo across ages: "I am the origin of the entire universe. Everything comes from Me. The wise, knowing this, worship Me with all their hearts."

In That Moment...

Kurukshetra was no longer just a battlefield. It had become a sacred classroom.

Arjuna sat, stunned—not in despair this time, but in awe. The Lord beside him was not merely divine; He was the source of divinity itself.

Everything—every element, every soul, every path—began and ended in Krishna.

And those who realised this truth were not ordinary. They had pierced through illusion, lifetimes of karma, layers of selfishness—and had come to see Krishna, not just in temples or idols, but in every leaf, every star, every breath.

KEY LESSONS FOR THE MODERN SEEKER

1. The divine is not distant.

God is not far away in the heavens—He is within everything. Look closely. The sacred hides in the simple: the taste that quenches thirst, the morning sunlight, the rhythm of your breath. Krishna is not absent from your life—He is your life.

2. You are His—always.

You are not a lost speck in a chaotic world. You are a spark of the Divine, a part of Krishna's own spiritual energy. Your existence has meaning because you belong to Him. Repeat in your heart, "I am Yours, Krishna," especially when you feel alone, anxious, or unworthy.

3. Few seek, fewer surrender—be one who does.

The spiritual path is not popular, and surrender is even rarer. But the rare ones are the dearest to Krishna. Be courageous enough to walk the quieter path of devotion—it leads straight to the heart of God.

4. Desire can distract—but Krishna fulfils.

Many seek pleasure, power, peace—but only Krishna gives Himself. Don't settle for drops of joy when you can dive into the ocean of divine love. Ask Krishna not for things, but for Himself. Say, "I want You, not just what You give."

5. To truly know Krishna takes lifetimes—but begin today.

Realising Krishna is the fruit of many lifetimes of hard work and prayers, but the journey starts now. Each act of sincerity, each moment of remembrance brings you closer. Don't wait for perfection—just begin. Whenever you feel overwhelmed, softly say: "Krishna, I may not understand everything yet, but I trust You."

Chapter 8

The Journey Beyond Death

The sun had dipped lower over Kurukshetra. Arjuna, now transformed into a seeker of truth, sat with a calm intensity. His mind stirred not with war strategies, but with deep, eternal questions.

"Krishna," he asked quietly, "what is Brahman? What is the self? What is karma? What is this material world really? Who is the Supreme Being who receives our offerings? And what happens at the time of death? How can someone reach you when they pass away from this world?"

Krishna's face shone with compassion. These were not questions of a warrior anymore—they were the questions of a soul searching for the ultimate meaning.

Krishna's voice, serene and all-knowing, began to flow like the sacred Ganges: "Arjuna, Brahman refers to the imperishable, eternal reality—the spirit that exists beyond this changing world. The ātmā, or the self, is the eternal individual soul. Karma refers to the actions that bind a soul to this world through reaction and rebirth."

He continued, painting the cosmic picture clearly: "This material world is ever-changing. But behind it all is My eternal nature. I am the Supreme Person, Purushottama, who resides in every heart, witnessing all actions, accepting all offerings, guiding every soul."

Arjuna listened, heart pounding. His question about death still lingered.

Krishna now turned to that most feared and mysterious transition.

"Those who remember Me at the time of death," He said, "come to Me. There is no doubt."

Arjuna's eyes widened. At death? When the body is failing? When the mind flickers like a dying flame—how can one remember God at that moment?

Krishna anticipated the thought.

"Whatever state of consciousness one remembers at death, that state they attain in the next life. Therefore, Arjuna, always try to remember Me to get into the habit. Think of Me and do your duty."

The battlefield came back into focus, but now seen through a divine lens. Fighting was no longer just a duty—it was a meditation.

Krishna pressed further: "Fix your mind upon Me. Offer your intelligence to Me. If you do this, without doubt, you will come to Me."

The secret was out: bhakti, pure devotion, was the path that transcended death.

Krishna revealed Himself again, this time not just as the charioteer or the friend, but as the Supreme Goal: "I am the Lord of the Vedas. I am the enjoyer of sacrifices. I am the goal of all yoga. I am the eternal seed of all beings. I am the imperishable."

And then He shared a vision of the soul's final journey.

Those who know the Supreme Truth, who remember Krishna in devotion, who have practised yoga sincerely—at the time of death, they exit through the crown of the head, their life-air rising with focused consciousness to the highest destination.

"They do not return to this mortal world," Krishna said. "They attain My eternal abode."

But for others, whose minds are not fixed, whose practices are distracted or incomplete—they may return again, bound by karma.

Arjuna's heart stirred again. Is there a difference in death itself?

Do the wise and the ordinary die the same way?

Krishna explained the two paths of the soul: one is the path of light—a soul who leaves the body in knowledge, in remembrance of the Lord, during auspicious times. That soul reaches the realm of no return.

The other is the path of darkness—one who dies in ignorance, whose mind is scattered or absorbed in worldly concerns. That soul returns to earthly life.

But Krishna added with grace: "These distinctions do not trouble My devotee. Whether light or dark, day or night, they transcend the cycle by My grace because their love is fixed on Me."

And then, as the chapter neared its end, Krishna made a promise more powerful than any reward of heaven: "Arjuna, the Vedas speak of great pleasures in the heavenly planets. But even those who reach heaven must return when their merits are exhausted."

"However, My devotee—who offers Me a leaf, a flower, a drop of water, or a sincere heart of love—never perishes. He comes to Me and stays with Me forever."

In That Moment...

The battlefield faded once more. In its place stood a grand highway of souls—some rising, some returning, some wandering.

And Arjuna? He now knew his destination.

Krishna was not merely a companion in life—He was the shelter at death, the goal beyond time, the love that dissolves all fear.

To remember Krishna at the time of death was not just a practice—it was the fruit of a life lived in devotion.

KEY LESSONS FOR THE MODERN SEEKER

1. Your final thought shapes forever.

The moment of death matters. Our final consciousness determines our next birth. Life is not just about how you live—but how you leave. What you think in your last breath becomes your next beginning. Train your mind now, so your last thought is your best thought.

2. Lock your mind on the divine GPS.

Those who remember Krishna at the final moment attain Him.

In the age of distractions, make Krishna your default setting. Where the mind runs at the end depends on where it rested all along. Daily remembrance = eternal destination.

3. Heart over habit: bhakti > ritual.

Devotion to Krishna brings eternal results; rituals give only temporary rewards. Don't get caught up in spiritual checklists. God reads your heart, not your calendar. A tear of love matters more than a thousand lamps offered with ego.

4. "The two roads after this life."

The path of light leads to freedom, the path of darkness to rebirth.

Life doesn't end at death—it splits. Every action now is voting for your next journey. Live with knowledge—clarity, truth, selflessness—and you'll rise beyond this cycle.

5. The devotee walks beyond time.

True devotees transcend karma and time; they return no more to this world of suffering.

Loving Krishna rewrites your fate. Devotion isn't escape—it's transcendence. When your soul anchors in divine love, even death bows before you.

Chapter 9

The Royal Secret

The sacred battlefield of Kurukshetra still rumbled in the distance. But on Arjuna's chariot, time itself seemed to stand still.

Krishna turned to Arjuna with a gaze full of affection—more personal than ever before.

"Arjuna," He said softly, "I am about to reveal to you the most confidential knowledge—the rāja-vidyā, the king of all knowledge, and the rāja-guhya, the king of secrets. It is pure, sublime, and brings immediate realisation. It is eternal, and easy to practise."

Arjuna's eyes lit up. A secret? From Krishna Himself?

Krishna leaned closer, His voice calm and kind.

"This knowledge is not for those who are envious, faithless, or indifferent. But because you are not like them—you are My dear friend and devotee—I shall reveal it to you."

And then came the secret, simple yet majestic: "All beings rest in Me, but I am not in them."

Arjuna blinked. How could that be?

Krishna explained, "Just as the wind blows within space, yet space remains unaffected, in the same way, all living beings are within Me, but I remain untouched."

"I create. I maintain. I destroy. Yet I remain above it all—ever sovereign."

And then Krishna revealed something that mystics and sages had pondered for lifetimes: "When the universe dissolves, all beings merge into My material nature. And when it is time again, I recreate them, again and again, according to their karma."

"But I don't desire anything," He added. "I simply act, like the wind moving the leaves—naturally through my energies, without attachment."

Arjuna's heart trembled. He had once known Krishna as his cousin, his charioteer. Now he saw Him as the eternal backdrop of all existence.

But Krishna was not finished.

"Fools deride Me when I descend in human form," He said, with both sorrow and dignity in His voice. "They do not know My supreme nature. They laugh at Me, thinking Me ordinary."

"They are bewildered by material nature, and they remain bound. But those who are wise—they worship Me with full heart."

And then Krishna spoke of His devotees, His beloved souls: "They constantly glorify Me. They bow down to Me. With minds fixed on Me, they serve Me with devotion—always."

"For them, I am the swift deliverer. I personally protect what they have and carry what they lack."

A divine warmth entered Krishna's voice.

"Even if one commits the most abominable acts, if they are devoted to Me with sincerity, they should be considered saintly. Because they are rightly situated. Soon, they become righteous and attain lasting peace."

Arjuna's breath caught. Even the fallen can rise through devotion?

Krishna answered with thunderous clarity: "Declare it boldly, O Arjuna: My devotee never perishes."

And then, He said something so beautiful, it would echo through time and scripture: "I am equal to all. I envy no one. But whoever worships Me with love—he is in Me, and I am in him."

Suddenly, the secret was not just a fact—it was a relationship. God was not distant or proud. He was personal, reachable… loving.

"Even those born into sinful or lower births, if they take shelter in Me, they too attain the supreme destination."

And as if speaking not only to Arjuna, but to every soul caught in the tides of this world, Krishna concluded: "Fix your mind on Me. Become My devotee. Worship Me. Offer your homage unto Me. If you do this, you will surely come to Me. This is My promise, Arjuna—for you are very dear to Me."

In That Moment…

Arjuna sat motionless. The battlefield, the noise, the warriors—all faded again.

This wasn't just knowledge—it was love. Krishna wasn't giving formulas or rituals. He was offering His very self.

This was the royal secret—not hidden in books, but hidden in devotion.

The Supreme Lord was not a force to fear—but a friend to trust, a father to return to, a beloved to serve.

Key Lessons for the Modern Seeker

1. Bhakti: the shortcut to the Lord.

Devotion is the supreme path. Even above knowledge or rituals, bhakti brings one directly to Krishna.

In a world obsessed with credentials and complexity, the path of love is still the most powerful. You don't need to master scriptures or rituals—just offer your heart sincerely. Bhakti is not the long way; it's the direct line to the Divine.

2. The hidden thread holding it all together.

Krishna is the source of everything. All beings rest in Him—even if they don't recognise it.

We may not see Him, but we stand on Him. Like Wi-Fi powering a device silently, Krishna sustains all life—consciously or not. True peace begins when you stop searching outside and start recognising the Source within.

3. Not partial. Just personal.

He is not partial, but personal. Krishna loves everyone equally but responds specially to those who love Him.

God doesn't play favourites, but He responds to feeling. Love opens the door to divine interaction. In a world where we crave validation, Krishna reminds us: You are seen, heard, and loved—especially when your love is real.

4. Grace is not about deserving—it's about surrendering.

Devotees are protected. Krishna ensures the spiritual success of anyone who surrenders to Him, regardless of background.

You don't have to be qualified—just willing. Your past doesn't disqualify you. Krishna isn't looking at your resumé; He's looking at your readiness. Surrender is the new success.

5. Divine guarantee: you're never alone.

"My devotee never perishes," is Krishna's personal assurance.

In a world of broken promises, here's one you can bank on. Krishna doesn't ghost, forget, or fail. His word is not just eternal—it's intimate. When you walk with Him, you're always carried, never abandoned.

Chapter 10

The Splendour of the Supreme

As the sun rose higher over the fields of Kurukshetra, Arjuna's eyes remained fixed on Krishna—not with the gaze of a warrior, but with the hunger of a soul yearning to know Him.

Krishna had already revealed Himself as the origin and shelter of all. But now, Arjuna longed to understand more—not just the truth of Krishna, but His greatness, His glory.

"O Krishna," Arjuna asked, his voice filled with reverence, "how can I know You in truth? In what forms should I meditate on You? Please describe Your divine opulence—Your manifestations in this world."

Krishna smiled, for this was the question of one whose heart was deeply rooted in love.

"My dear Arjuna," He began, "because you are My dear friend, I shall speak further—for your joy and benefit."

And then, in words that shimmered like rays of sunlight through clouds, Krishna spoke the truth of His greatness: "I am the origin of all—everything emanates from Me. The wise, knowing this, worship Me with all their hearts."

Arjuna's breath caught. Everything?

Krishna nodded. "Yes, those who know this truth engage in My devotional service. They speak of Me with joy, their minds absorbed in Me, their souls satisfied by Me."

And then Krishna gave a rare glimpse into the secret of His mercy: "To those who are constantly devoted, who worship Me with love—I give the knowledge by which they can come to Me."

"But more than that," He added, "out of compassion, I dwell within their hearts. With the lamp of knowledge, I destroy the darkness of ignorance."

This was not the God of far-off heavens. This was the Lord who walks with His devotee, who guides from within.

Arjuna's voice trembled. "Krishna, I now know that You are the Supreme Lord—eternal, beyond birth, the shelter of all that is. All the great sages confirm this, and now I too accept it without doubt."

He folded his hands in devotion. "Please, Krishna, describe again—how are You present in all things? How shall I meditate on You amidst the wonders of this world?"

Krishna's smile widened. "Very well, Arjuna. I shall speak—not in full, for My glories are endless—but I will describe some of My divine opulences. Hear now."

And then, like a cosmic thunder rolling through creation, Krishna revealed:

"Among the Adityas, I am Vishnu.

Among lights, I am the radiant sun.

Of the Maruts, I am Marīchi. Among stars, I am the moon.

Of the Vedas, I am the Sama Veda.

Of the gods, I am Indra, the king of heaven.

Of weapons, I am the thunderbolt.

Of mountains, I am Meru.

Of priests, I am Brihaspati.

Of generals, I am Skanda.

Of bodies of water, I am the ocean."

Arjuna listened, heart lifted with wonder. This was no longer philosophy—it was Krishna alive in everything.

Krishna continued:

"Among purifiers, I am the wind.

Of warriors, I am Rama.

Among beasts, I am the lion.

Of birds, I am Garuda, the king of flight.

Of creations, I am the beginning, the end, and the middle."

Each word unfolded a universe within a universe.

And Krishna spoke still more:

"Among trees, I am the banyan.

Among sages, I am Narada.

Among celestial musicians, I am Chitraratha.

Among perfected beings, I am Kapila, the sage of divine wisdom.

Of seasons, I am spring, the flowery, joyful one."

And then Krishna revealed the deeper thread tying it all together: "There is no being—moving or non-moving—that can exist without Me. All forms, all strengths, all beauty in this world—are just sparkles of My splendour."

Krishna concluded gently: "What need is there, Arjuna, for all this detailed knowledge? I am seated in the hearts of all beings. By a single fragment of Myself, I pervade and support this entire universe."

In That Moment…

Arjuna closed his eyes—not in sleep, but in stillness.

He no longer had to imagine the divine. He saw Krishna in the rising sun, in the wind that brushed across his skin, in the lion's roar, the river's flow, the stars above, and the silence between thoughts.

Krishna was not just in the universe. The universe was but a shadow of His brilliance.

And now, Arjuna's meditation had direction—not just toward the formless Absolute, but toward the Supreme Person, whose every aspect was saturated with meaning and majesty.

Key Lessons for the Modern Seeker

1. The source code: Krishna behind it all.

Krishna is the source of everything. All beauty, strength, intelligence, and glory reflect His splendour.

Like a hidden source code powers every app, Krishna powers every talent, moment of brilliance, and spark of beauty. When you admire someone's genius, strength, or charisma—pause and remember the divine origin. Shift from admiration to adoration.

2. "Wi-Fi to wisdom: devotion unlocks divine signal."

Devotion brings revelation. To those who love Krishna, He gives the knowledge to come to Him.

Just like Wi-Fi needs a password, divine truth needs a connection—and that password is love. Sincere devotion clears the fog of confusion and downloads spiritual clarity.

Don't just study God—love Him.

3. God is not a vibe—He's a person.

God is personal. Krishna is not an abstract force—He is a person who responds to love.

In a world full of "the Universe will provide" quotes, Krishna offers something deeper: a personal relationship. You can talk to Him, laugh with Him, cry to Him. He's not energy—He's eternally yours. Real spirituality starts with real connection.

4. The divine within: you're never alone.

Krishna dwells within all. He lives in the heart of every being and sustains the entire cosmos with just a part of Himself.

We don't have to look out to find God—He's right in you. That still, loving voice in your heart? That's Him. Every breath is proof you're powered by the Divine. Turn inward—not to escape, but to meet Krishna.

5. Turn the world into a temple.

The world can be a window to the divine. By seeing Krishna in all things, the material becomes spiritual.

Your life doesn't need an escape—it needs a lens. A cup of chai, a sunset, your best friend's laughter—see Krishna's beauty and presence in it all, and you've just stepped into a sacred space.

Don't run from the world—reveal Krishna in it.

Chapter 11

The Vision That Shook the Universe

The air was heavy with silence on the battlefield of Kurukshetra. The warriors, chariots, and flags seemed to fade into the background as Arjuna turned to Krishna, his charioteer, guide, and dearest friend.

"Krishna," Arjuna said, eyes filled with deep reverence, "You have spoken to me of Your glories—how You are the Supreme, the origin of all, the eternal guardian of dharma. I believe You. But… I long to see this truth."

His voice trembled with the weight of his request.

"If You think I am worthy, O Lord," he continued, "please show me Your divine form—not this human-like form I see before me, but the real You, the Universal Form, as You stand beyond time and space."

Krishna smiled gently. "My dear Arjuna," He said, "behold what no one has seen before—not sages, nor gods. You are blessed, and so I shall grant you divine vision. With these eyes of flesh, My eternal form cannot be perceived. But now… prepare yourself."

In that instant, the air cracked with energy. Arjuna's eyes widened, his heart raced.

Before him, Krishna began to transform.

What emerged was no longer the dark-hued, flute-playing friend of Vrindavan. No—it was the Vishvarupa, the Universal Form. A radiant, boundless being with countless faces, arms, eyes, and ornaments. Infinite weapons gleamed from His many hands. Garlands of heavenly flowers adorned His neck, and robes of cosmic splendour swirled around Him.

Everywhere Arjuna looked, he saw Krishna. In every direction—past, present, and future—He was all-encompassing. Suns blazed from His eyes, galaxies rotated on His shoulders, and the chant of Om reverberated in the ether like the hum of creation itself.

Arjuna's knees gave way. He folded his hands in awe.

In the body of Krishna, he saw the celestial gods—the gods of wind, fire, rain, and sun—bowing in submission. He saw sages offering hymns of praise. But he also saw destruction: great warriors like Bhishma, Drona, and Karna being devoured by a fierce fire emerging from Krishna's many mouths.

Arjuna cried out, shaken.

"Who are You in this terrifying form?" he asked, his voice barely audible. "Why do You consume all directions with flame and fury?"

And Krishna replied, His voice echoing like thunder: "I am Kaala—the destroyer of worlds. I have come to annihilate all those who stand against dharma. Whether you fight or not, the fate of these warriors is already sealed. Arise, Arjuna! Be but an instrument of My will and take the credit."

Arjuna's head bowed low, his pride shattered.

He realised he was no longer merely a prince or warrior—he was a chosen instrument of the Divine Plan.

With trembling devotion, he prayed, "O Lord of infinite power, I did not know Your true glory. I called You 'friend' and joked with You… forgive me! You are the shelter of the universe. Show me once more Your gentle, loving form."

Hearing this sincere plea, Krishna withdrew the Universal Form. The terrifying flames vanished. First Krishna transformed into a four-handed form of Vishnu and then into His original beautiful, compassionate form of Shyamasundara—the smiling, flute-bearing form of Krishna that had enchanted the gopis of Vrindavan.

Seeing Him thus, Arjuna sighed with relief. Peace washed over his soul.

Krishna spoke softly, "Arjuna, not by Vedic study, severe penance, or ritual can one see Me in My original Form. But through bhakti—pure devotion—I can be known, seen, and entered into."

The winds of Kurukshetra resumed their rhythm. The battle still awaited.

But something had shifted. Arjuna was no longer the confused warrior who had once dropped his bow. He had seen the infinite. He had bowed before the Supreme.

He was ready.

KEY LESSONS FOR THE MODERN SEEKER

1. When God revealed the multiverse.

Truth isn't limited to what the senses perceive. Just like Arjuna needed divine vision to see the Universal Form, we too need inner awakening to grasp reality beyond the physical.

Don't reduce the divine to a form that fits your comfort zone. True vision requires surrender, not just sight.

2. From friend to forever: when Arjuna saw the truth.

We often approach God casually—until He shows us who He truly is. Arjuna's shift from calling Krishna "friend" to bowing in reverence mirrors our journey from spiritual curiosity to heartfelt devotion.

Familiarity with God should never breed forgetfulness of His greatness.

3. The day the Universe spoke.

Krishna didn't *speak* the cosmos—He *became* it. In a world chasing cosmic experiences through psychedelics or space theories, the *Gita* offers a timeless truth: the universe is not just outside us—it's *Him*.

True cosmic consciousness isn't found in stars but in surrender.

4. Crushed ego, awakened soul.

When Krishna revealed His fierce form, Arjuna's ego shattered. Only then did he become a true servant of dharma. The path to purpose often begins with the end of pride.

Life breaks us to awaken us. Let your breakdown be your breakthrough.

5. Bhakti > everything.

Not penance. Not rituals. Not even scholarship. Only bhakti—loving devotion—grants access to Krishna's sweetest form.

In a world of performance, God still looks at the heart. Choose love over achievement.

Chapter 12

The Path of Devotion

The cosmic form had faded.

Krishna now stood again in His most beautiful, two-armed form—radiant, smiling, with lotus eyes full of affection.

Arjuna, whose heart had just been thunderstruck by the vision of the Universal Form, now sat quietly. There was awe in his soul, yes—but above all, there was love.

And now, a new question arose in him—not of war, not of fear, but of devotion.

"O Krishna," he asked gently, "some people worship You as the personal God, in form, with love and surrender. Others worship the impersonal Brahman—the unmanifested, eternal energy or formless aspect. Which of these is superior?"

Krishna looked at Arjuna with a smile that carried timeless understanding.

"Those who fix their minds on Me, My form with unwavering love," He said, "who worship Me with full devotion—offering body, mind, and heart—they are most perfect in My eyes."

"But," He added, "those who try to reach Me by meditating on the form—on the unmanifested Brahman—the path is much harder. Their progress is filled with struggle, for it is very difficult to develop love for that which has no form, no qualities."

Arjuna listened closely. This was the essence of all paths laid bare.

Krishna continued, His voice now as soft as sandalwood: "But for those who worship Me, who surrender all actions to Me, who meditate upon Me, fixing their minds on Me without deviation—I become their swift deliverer from the ocean of birth and death."

It was not intellect, not renunciation, not austerity, but loving surrender that brought the soul to the Supreme.

"Just fix your mind on Me," Krishna said, "and be devoted to Me. Worship Me. Offer your homage to Me. You will come to Me. This I promise you—because you are very dear to Me."

Arjuna bowed his head. But what of those who could not fix the mind so fully? Were they lost?

Krishna answered with kindness: "If you cannot fix your mind on

Me entirely, then practise remembering Me regularly (by setting up a daily discipline of spiritual practices). Train your heart through spiritual discipline."

"If even that is too difficult, then simply work for Me. Offer the results of your actions to Me. That too will bring you perfection."

"And if you cannot do that," He said, "then renounce the fruits of your work—act without selfish expectation. That too purifies the soul."

Krishna was building a staircase to Himself—for every soul, at every level.

And then, the Lord described the qualities that make a devotee truly dear to Him—not birth, not caste, not scholarship—but the qualities of the heart:

"One who does not hate any being, who is friendly and compassionate…

Who is free from pride, possessiveness, and ego…

Who remains steady in pain and pleasure…

Who is forgiving, content, self-controlled, and engaged in Me with determination…

Who disturbs no one, and is not disturbed by others…

Who is silent, humble, and pure of heart…

Who has no expectations, who is fixed in devotion, unshaken by honour or dishonour…"

One by one, Krishna revealed the qualities that shine brighter than jewels in the heart of a true devotee.

And finally, He declared with divine assurance: "One who follows this path of devotion, who serves Me with faith, who makes Me their only goal—that devotee is exceedingly dear to Me."

In That Moment…

The battlefield of Kurukshetra faded again—not in sound, but in importance.

What mattered now was not victory in war, but victory over the false self.

Arjuna realised that love—not power or intellect—was the highest path.

And Krishna, the Lord of all universes, was not demanding perfection, but offering it—to anyone willing to serve with a sincere heart.

The *Gita's* secret shone in full: bhakti, loving devotional service, is the highest yoga.

KEY LESSONS FOR THE MODERN SEEKER

1. Heart over hype.

Personal devotion is supreme. Worshipping Krishna with love and surrender is the highest path.

In a world chasing aesthetics and show, God is moved by sincerity—not performance. The truest spiritual upgrade is not in louder chants or fancier altars, but in a heart that whispers, "I am Yours."

2. He meets you where you are.

Krishna is merciful. He meets each soul where they are, offering many levels of approach.

You don't have to be perfect to begin. Whether you're broken, curious, or sceptical—Krishna doesn't expect perfection. He honours intention. Start wherever you are, and He'll walk the path with you.

3. No labels, just love.

Bhakti is not limited. Anyone can become dear to Krishna, regardless of background.

Spiritual connection isn't gated by race, gender, caste, or credentials. It's about the soul, not the résumé. The door to Krishna's heart is open to all—no judgement, just genuine love.

4. Vibes don't lie—character counts.

The qualities of a true devotee matter most: humility, compassion, steadiness, and purity.

Spiritual clout isn't built on loud quotes or ritual routines—it's about how you live, love, and lift others. A humble, kind soul is more elevated than a proud scholar.

5. It's not the size, it's the sincerity.

Krishna wants the heart. The simplest offering of love is more precious than the grandest ritual without devotion.

Don't wait to "have more" to give something to God. A flower, a tear, a heartfelt word—even these can move the Divine more than gold-plated grandeur. It's the intention that counts.

Chapter 13

The Hidden Owner of the Body

The sun was shining bright. The air held the weight of silence. It was a moment suspended in time—no arrows flew, no war drums echoed. On a grand chariot in the middle of the battlefield, Arjuna, the great warrior, sat in deep thought.

He turned toward Krishna, who held the reins of the horses with effortless grace. Arjuna's voice was soft but intense.

"O Keshava, You have spoken about the soul, about matter, and about transcendence. But there's something more I long to understand. Please tell me—what is this body? Who am I really? What is nature? Who is the enjoyer? What is true knowledge?"

Krishna, the Supreme Lord, smiled gently, His eyes reflecting compassion and divine wisdom.

"O Arjuna," He began, "this body of yours—indeed, every

body—is like a field. And the one who experiences this body, who lives within it and observes its changes, is the knower of the field—the soul."

Arjuna listened attentively.

"But there is something even more wondrous," Krishna continued. "I am the knower in all bodies. I am the Supersoul, seated in every heart. I witness all thoughts, guide all beings, yet I remain untouched by the body's actions."

Arjuna's heart stirred. This was unlike any knowledge he had heard before. Krishna was not just his charioteer—He was the eternal observer in all living entities.

The Body Is the Field, the Soul Is the Knower

Krishna now painted a divine picture with words.

"Think of this body as a field. It is made of earth, water, fire, air, and ether. It also includes the mind, intelligence, and false ego. Within this field dwell the senses, desires, thoughts of happiness and distress, love and hatred. All these are the ingredients of material existence."

"And the soul? The soul is you, Arjuna. Not your name, not your title, but the spark of consciousness that shines within you. That soul is eternal. But alongside that soul, I dwell as the Supersoul, watching, guiding, and loving."

Krishna's voice now carried a gentle urgency.

"My dear Arjuna, let Me tell you what real knowledge is—not bookish scholarship, but the wisdom that opens the eyes of the soul."

And He began to list the qualities of the truly wise: "Humility, nonviolence, tolerance, simplicity, cleanliness, self-control, detachment from temporary pleasures, the ability to see the miseries of birth, death, old age, and disease…"

"Even-mindedness in joy and sorrow, constant and unalloyed devotion to Me, living simply, avoiding crowds, seeking the truth, and surrendering to a spiritual teacher—these, Arjuna, are the signs of knowledge. All else is ignorance."

Arjuna felt something shift in his heart. He realised that spiritual vision wasn't about pride or complexity—it was about purity, simplicity, and connection to Krishna.

Now Krishna revealed something even more intimate.

"The soul is real," He said, "but beyond even the soul is the knowable truth—Me. I am Brahman, the Absolute Truth, eternal and beyond cause and effect. Though I am unseen, I am everywhere."

"My hands and legs are everywhere. My eyes, ears, heads and faces are everywhere. I see all, I hear all, I sustain all, yet I remain detached. I am the Supersoul, the silent witness within every being."

He spoke with calm conviction: "Though I appear to be divided among all beings, I am never divided. I am the light of all lights. I reside in every heart, and I am the source, the object, and the goal of all knowledge."

Arjuna was stunned—not in fear, but in awe. The One sitting before him on the chariot was the very source of all consciousness. He had never heard anyone make such claims. He had no reason to not believe.

Krishna now explained the origin of all suffering.

"Arjuna, this material world has no beginning. Nature and the soul have always existed. But it is nature—the field—that causes the body to act, and it is the soul that experiences the results."

"The living entity becomes entangled when he forgets his spiritual identity and tries to enjoy the material field living a Godless life. Depending on his desires and actions, he takes birth again and again—sometimes as a demigod, sometimes as an animal, sometimes as a human. This is samsara, the cycle of birth and death."

"But within this body, alongside the soul, is another—a silent witness, the Lord, the supreme enjoyer. He is the overseer, the guide, the permitter who sanctions everyone's desires. That is Me—the Paramatma, the Supersoul."

Krishna's voice softened.

"When one truly understands this—that nature acts, the soul experiences, and I oversee—such a person becomes free. He need not take birth again. He is liberated."

In That Moment…

Arjuna closed his eyes. The battlefield faded. He now saw the world within.

Krishna now described the different paths people take: "Some reach Me through deep meditation. Others through selfless work. Some simply hear about Me from sincere devotees and, by hearing, their hearts awaken. Even they transcend death."

He paused.

"Whatever exists in this world—whether walking or still—is but a combination of the body and the soul. But one who sees Me, the Supersoul, equally present in all beings, that person sees truly."

"When you realise," Krishna said, "that all actions are done by the body under material nature, and that the soul does nothing—then you are wise."

"The soul, like the sky, is never touched by anything—even though it seems surrounded by clouds. Similarly, the wise soul is untouched by the body."

"Just as the sun illuminates the whole world, consciousness spreads throughout the body and reveals life. That consciousness comes from the soul, the source of life."

Krishna now gave the final jewel of wisdom: "One who sees the difference between the body and the soul, and who understands how the soul can be liberated from material nature—such a person attains Me."

For Arjuna, it was the dawn of something wonderful. He had begun this chapter seeking knowledge of the body and the soul—but what he received was the key to liberation, and the most intimate glimpse into the heart of God.

KEY LESSONS FOR THE MODERN SEEKER

1. You are not the body—you are the knower within.

You are not your job, your face, or even your thoughts. You are the conscious witness—the soul—inhabiting this temporary body. Real peace begins the moment you stop identifying with the changing and start connecting with the unchanging within.

You're not your LinkedIn bio or your selfie. You're the eternal soul behind it all. Start investing in your inner life.

2. There's a silent partner in your heart.

You're not navigating life alone. Krishna, the Supersoul, dwells within you—guiding, witnessing, and loving you unconditionally. Listen inward. The truest voice is already there.

You don't need to Google all your answers—try inner Wi-Fi. Divine GPS is already installed.

3. True knowledge isn't about information—it's about transformation.

Humility, simplicity, devotion, and self-control—these are not just virtues; they are doorways to higher consciousness. It's not about how much you know, but how much you live that matters.

Life isn't a trivia contest. Growth happens when wisdom turns into lifestyle, not just status updates.

4. See the soul, not the shell.

Wisdom is when you stop seeing people by race, status, or appearance—and start seeing the equal presence of God in every heart. Real vision begins with spiritual eyes.

Swipe past the outer layers. Everyone you meet is a soul on a journey—just like you.

5. Liberation comes from realising who does what.

The body acts, nature drives, the soul experiences, and God permits. When you understand this divine arrangement, you stop blaming, stop clinging—and start living with freedom, clarity, and surrender.

You don't have to control everything. Know your role. Do your part. Let the universe breathe. We are not the ones running it.

Chapter 14

The Three Invisible Chains

The battlefield of Kurukshetra now lay veiled in full sunlight. Arjuna sat near Krishna, eyes wide with wonder. Each answer from Krishna had not only solved a question but unlocked new realms of mystery. The truths of the soul, the Supersoul, and liberation stirred something deep within him.

But he had one more question.

"O Krishna," he said softly, "You've explained the soul and the material world… but what keeps the soul bound here? What are the forces that make us act—sometimes gently, sometimes violently, sometimes wisely, and other times foolishly? Please tell me."

Krishna, the Supreme Lord, turned to him with a serene smile.

"My dear Arjuna," He said, "hear now of the three modes of

material nature—sattva (goodness), rajas (passion), and tamas (ignorance). These are like three ropes, binding the eternal soul to the temporary body. Though the soul is divine, these modes condition it to forget Me."

The First Chain—Sattva (Goodness)

"Goodness, O Arjuna," Krishna said, "is the purest mode. It shines like a crystal. When someone lives in this mode or leads a sattvic life, their heart becomes calm, their mind becomes clear, and their actions are gentle and wise. Such a person feels happiness not from indulgence, but from understanding, charity, humility, and peace."

"But," Krishna warned, "even goodness is a chain. It binds one with pride and attachment to virtue and knowledge. One may enjoy the light of the higher realms, but without surrender to Me, even that soul remains in the cycle of birth and death."

The Second Chain—Rajas (Passion)

Krishna's tone shifted as He spoke of the next mode.

"Passion is like fire," He said. "It binds the soul with ropes of desire and action. Those in rajas are always chasing—wealth, power, pleasures, fame. Their minds are never still, their hearts never satisfied."

"Though they may achieve great things, they are constantly

disturbed by longing and anxiety. At the end of life, one influenced by passion is born again among those addicted to work and material ambition."

Arjuna nodded, recognising the restless nature Krishna described.

The Third Chain—Tamas (Ignorance)

Then Krishna described the darkest rope.

"Tamas, Arjuna, is ignorance. It is like a heavy fog that covers the soul's vision. It brings laziness, illusion, and madness. Those in tamas prefer sleep to effort, delusion to truth, destruction over creation."

"They do not know what to do or what not to do. They live without purpose, and at the time of death, they descend into lower forms of life."

Krishna looked into Arjuna's eyes.

"These three modes, though subtle, influence every action, every thought. No one in the material world is free from their grip—not even the greatest of scholars or kings. They flow through the food we eat, the company we keep, the words we speak, the dreams we chase. Everything in this world falls under these three modes. Every time we make a choice, we condition ourselves to the mode that choice falls under."

"But," He said with a divine gleam, "those who take shelter in

Me—by engaging in devotional service—can rise above these modes. They are not pulled by lust, anger, laziness, or even pride. They are like a lotus in the water—untouched, serene, free."

Arjuna asked eagerly, "How can I recognise such a soul, O Krishna? What does he look like? How does he live?"

Krishna replied: "Such a person doesn't get shaken by moods—whether it's a high-energy day, a lazy one, or a confused mess."

"He does not chase the highs or fear the lows. He stays calm, knowing that 'just the modes are active—not the real me'."

"Pleasure and pain, honour and dishonour, praise and blame—he treats them all the same."

"He serves Me with unwavering devotion. He depends on Me alone. Such a person is beyond the influence of the modes. He reaches My eternal realm."

Then Krishna, with great compassion, revealed the essence of the chapter: "I am the source of the spiritual world. I am beyond the modes."

"All conditioned souls are struggling in My material energy, but those who take shelter of My lotus feet, by devotional service, cross this vast ocean of illusion."

"They do not take birth again. They come to live with Me eternally."

As the words flowed from Krishna's lips, Arjuna felt the knots in his heart begin to loosen. The three modes were no longer just philosophical concepts—they were real, and he could feel them pulling on his mind. But now, he also saw the way out.

Key Lessons for the Modern Seeker

1. Even good vibes can be a trap.

Living in *sattva*—calmness, mindfulness, and ethical living—is better than chaos, but still not enough. Pride in our "goodness" can quietly trap us in ego.

Don't get stuck in the spiritual comfort zone. Growth doesn't end with wellness routines or kindness. Go beyond virtue—seek deep connection with the Divine.

2. Hustle culture is a golden cage.

Rajas binds us through ambition and desire. Always running, never arriving.

You might crush your goals, but if your inner peace is missing, it's just burnout dressed as success. Pause. Reflect. Ask: Is this serving my soul or just my image?

3. Comfort can be a silent killer.

Tamas dulls the soul. Laziness, distraction, apathy—these are the chains of spiritual sleep.

Doomscrolling, numbing out, and giving in to confusion aren't harmless habits—they're signs we're stuck in the fog. Wake up before life passes by unnoticed.

4. The mode you're in shapes the life you live.

The food you eat, the content you consume, the people around you—they all shift your consciousness into *sattva*, *rajas*, or *tamas*.

Your environment is programming you. Be intentional. Choose clarity over clutter, stillness over stimulation, service over self-obsession.

5. The way out: don't fight the chains—transcend them.

You can't beat the modes by willpower alone. But by taking shelter in Krishna—through love, devotion, and surrender—you rise above them.

True freedom isn't found in control—it's found in connection. Anchor your life in devotion, and you'll float like a lotus—untouched by the chaos.

Chapter 15

The Upside-Down Tree

Streaks of blue coloured the sky. The cool morning breeze whispered over the sleeping battlefield. Arjuna, still seated with Krishna on the chariot, felt as though he was standing on the edge of two worlds—the visible and the invisible.

Krishna looked at him and began to speak again, His voice calm and resonant.

"Arjuna, let Me show you something rare… something that wise souls have seen only through the eyes of devotion."

"There is a tree," Krishna said, "unlike any tree you've seen. Its roots grow upward, and its branches stretch downward. Upon its branches hang the Vedic hymns like leaves, and its fruits are the experiences of this world—pleasure and pain, success and failure."

Arjuna's brow furrowed in curiosity.

"This is the Banyan tree of material existence," Krishna explained. "It grows from the desire to enjoy separately from Me. It reflects eternal reality in a twisted, inverted form—just like a tree reflected on the surface of water."

"The branches of this tree are nourished by the three modes—goodness, passion, and ignorance. Its twigs are the objects of the senses, and its roots—growing down into illusion—are embedded in selfish actions and repeated birth and death."

Krishna paused, then said gravely: "This tree, Arjuna, must be cut down—not with an axe, but with the weapon of detachment. Only then can one escape the maze of material illusion and seek the true shelter—Me."

Arjuna wondered, "But if we leave this world, where does everyone go?"

Krishna, reading Arjuna's mind, replied: "After cutting down the tree of illusion, one must search for that place where life is eternal—My supreme abode, from which no one returns. That world is not lit by sun, moon, or fire. It is self-effulgent. It is My divine realm."

Krishna replied, "Know this, Arjuna—I am the eternal seed of all beings. A tiny part of Me becomes the living entity. That soul carries the mind and senses with it from one body to the next, just as air carries fragrance from one flower to another."

"When the soul enters a new body, it receives new senses. When it departs, those senses leave with it. Though unseen, the soul animates the body, giving it life and consciousness."

Arjuna listened in excitement.

Krishna now revealed His omnipresence: "I am the fire of digestion in all living beings. I enter into each body and help to digest the four kinds of food."

"I am seated in everyone's heart. From Me come memory, knowledge, and forgetfulness."

"I am the compiler of the Vedas, the knower of the Vedas, and the goal of the Vedas."

"Everything rests upon Me, yet I am beyond all."

Arjuna sat still, his heart filled with awe. He had known Krishna as a friend, a cousin, even a charioteer. But now he saw Him as the eternal origin, the One who sustains the entire creation with love and detachment.

Krishna now explained something profound.

"There are two kinds of beings in this world—the fallible and the infallible. The fallible are all living beings in the material world, bound by ignorance. The infallible are those perfected beings who reside in the spiritual realm, free from illusion."

"But beyond both," Krishna said with divine authority, "is the

Supreme Person—Me—the original source, the eternal Lord. I pervade and support both the spiritual and material realms. That is why I am known as Purushottama, the Supreme Person."

Krishna leaned forward slightly.

"Arjuna, this knowledge is the most secret of all. Whoever understands this wisdom becomes truly wise. Such a soul knows the real purpose of life. They do not waste their existence chasing shadows."

And with that, Krishna's words settled like sacred dust upon the heart of Arjuna.

Key Lessons for the Modern Seeker

1. The inverted tree: don't be fooled by the reflection.

The material world is like an upside-down tree—what seems real is actually a reflection, not the source.

In a world of curated feeds and filtered lives, don't mistake appearance for truth. Seek the root, not just the reflection. Real fulfilment lies beyond surface success.

2. Cut the tree with detachment.

To escape the entanglement of illusion, one must cut down the material tree with the sword of detachment.

Let go of toxic attachments, unhealthy habits, and ego-driven goals. Detachment doesn't mean indifference—it means choosing what truly nourishes the soul over what merely stimulates the senses.

3. You are not this body.

The soul is a part of Krishna, travelling from one body to another, carrying its desires like wind carrying scent.

You are more than your body, status, or social identity. Discover the unchanging *you* beneath life's changing roles—and let that self-guide your choices.

4. Krishna is within you.

Krishna resides in the heart of every being, giving memory, knowledge, and forgetfulness.

Tune in. Your inner voice, your conscience, that spark of insight in stillness—that's not random. It's Krishna guiding from within. Listen more. Surrender more.

5. Know the Supreme Person.

Beyond all dualities lies Purushottama—Krishna, the Supreme Person, the goal of all spiritual pursuit.

Life isn't just about survival or success. It's about connection with the Source. In a chaotic world, align with Krishna—the centre that never shifts.

Arjuna leaned in.

The Divine Qualities: Jewels of the Soul

Krishna's voice was like the morning sun rising—warm, illuminating, and pure.

"The divine qualities are like garlands worn by saintly souls. They spring from goodness and devotion. These are their signs:

— Fearlessness in spiritual life

— Purity of heart

— Steady pursuit of knowledge

— Charity without expectation

— Control of the senses

— Performance of sacrifice

— Study of the scriptures

— Austerity and simplicity

— Truthfulness

— Compassion toward all beings

— Peacefulness, modesty, forgiveness

— Absence of pride, envy, and attachment

— Devotion to Me without deviation.

Chapter 16

The Divine and the Demoniac

The silence of Kurukshetra was heavy with meaning. The sun witnessed the sacred conversation still unfolding on Arjuna's chariot. Arjuna had heard of the soul, the body, the three modes, and the path to transcendence. Yet a question lingered in his heart.

"Krishna," he asked softly, "why do some people live with purity, peace, and devotion while others act cruelly, arrogantly, and selfishly? What makes a soul divine—and what makes one demoniac?"

Krishna, the Supreme Lord, began to speak—not just to answer Arjuna, but to awaken the whole world.

"There are two kinds of beings, O son of Pritha," Krishna said, "the divine and the demoniac. The divine path leads to liberation, the demoniac to bondage. Now hear from Me in detail."

These qualities arise in those whose hearts are open to Me. Such people live not for their own pleasure, but for the welfare of all—and for My satisfaction."

The Demoniac Nature: Chains of Darkness

Then Krishna's tone changed—still calm, but firm and clear.

"But Arjuna, know also of the demoniac qualities—born of ignorance, pride, and envy. These souls do not follow scripture or higher guidance. They believe the world is without order, without God, and that life has no goal beyond sense gratification."

Krishna described them vividly: "They are arrogant, harsh, self-centred, intoxicated by false prestige. Driven by endless desires, they work hard for power, not for peace."

"They think, 'This is mine. I have conquered this. I will enjoy more. I am perfect. I am the master. Who else is there like me?' Bewildered by ego, they forget Me, the Supreme Lord in their hearts."

"They offer no sacrifice, no devotion. They take shelter of lust and greed. And, thus, they fall deeper into illusion, birth after birth."

Arjuna's heart trembled. The contrast was sharp. What becomes of these souls?

Krishna explained: "The divine soul walks the path of light and gradually reaches Me."

"The demoniac soul, chained by ignorance and sinful acts, descends into lower births—into wombs of darkness. They suffer again and again, lost in delusion."

"But," Krishna added with compassion, "no one is born eternally divine or demoniac. Every soul can rise, if only they turn toward Me."

But how? Arjuna wondered.

Krishna now revealed the key.

"Arjuna, how should one know what to do and what not to do? One must follow shastra—the sacred scriptures. Not personal whim, not social trend, not temporary pleasure. The scriptures are My voice in written form."

He concluded: "One who disregards scriptural instructions and acts according to his own desires does not attain perfection, happiness, or the Supreme Goal."

"But one who shapes his life according to My word, who performs his duties in surrender and devotion—that person becomes perfect, finds peace, and reaches Me."

As Krishna's words echoed into the thick morning air, Arjuna sat silently. Within him, a light was forming—not the fire of weapons or war, but the flame of discrimination. He now saw clearly:

Divine and demoniac are not races or appearances.

They are tendencies, choices, qualities of the heart.

A divine life is not inherited—it is cultivated.

A demoniac nature is not fixed—it can be purified.

And the key to both is one's attitude toward Krishna.

KEY LESSONS FOR THE MODERN SEEKER

1. Your character is your destiny.

Krishna says divine and demoniac qualities are not inherited—they are cultivated.

It's not your background, looks, or labels that define you—but your values, habits, and how you treat others. Your daily choices carve the path to peace or chaos. Choose well.

2. Spiritual life requires fearless integrity.

Fearlessness in spiritual life is the first divine quality Krishna lists.

In a world driven by trends, it takes courage to live with spiritual integrity. Speak truth, practise compassion, and stay rooted even if it's unpopular. That's real strength.

3. Ego is the real enemy.

Demoniac souls are trapped by pride, greed, and delusion of control.

"I, me, mine" thinking destroys peace. The more you chase status, control, and comparison, the more you suffer. Let go of ego; embrace humility. That's where joy begins.

4. Scripture over social media.

Krishna warns against acting on whims or social trends without scriptural guidance.

Don't let trending reels or influencers define your life's meaning. Let sacred wisdom guide your actions. The *Gita* isn't outdated—it's your inner GPS for clarity in a noisy world.

5. Everyone has a choice to rise.

No soul is permanently divine or demoniac—change is possible through turning to Krishna.

Your past doesn't limit your future. Even if you've messed up, you can reset. Surrender to a higher purpose, take the shelter of truth, and start your divine journey—today.

Chapter 17

The Shape of Your Faith

As the sacred dialogue between Krishna and Arjuna continued under the skies of Kurukshetra, Arjuna's mind turned toward the many people he had seen in his life—some sincere but not scripturally trained, some austere yet harsh, some charitable yet proud. His heart sought clarity.

He folded his palms and asked gently, "O Krishna, what about those who worship with faith, but not exactly according to the scriptures? Are their actions in the mode of goodness, passion, or ignorance?"

Krishna, the Supreme Lord, smiled at the sincerity behind the question.

"O Arjuna," He began, "faith is not one single thing. It takes shape based on the nature a person has developed. And nature, as you now know, is governed by the three modes—goodness, passion, and ignorance. According to one's dominant mode, their faith also changes."

Faith: A Mirror of the Heart

Krishna explained that faith is like a mirror reflecting one's inner condition. Whatever mode influences a person, that becomes the flavour of their worship.

"Those in the mode of goodness worship the demigods—beings of light, intelligence, and cosmic service."

"Those in the mode of passion worship power-hungry spirits and ambitious personalities—motivated by desire and ego."

"And those in ignorance turn to ghosts, dark forces, and strange rituals, often harming themselves or others in the name of worship."

Austerity Without Compassion

Krishna went deeper.

"There are some who perform severe austerities—starving themselves, torturing their bodies—not out of love for Me, but driven by pride and desire or sometimes not knowing why they are doing it. They disregard scripture and hurt even the Supersoul dwelling within."

Such persons, Krishna declared, are acting not divinely, but demonically. True austerity is not about punishment—it's about purification.

"Spiritual life is not self-harm. Fasting, simplicity, and restraint are meant to purify, not punish. If our practice is making us bitter or hard-hearted, we must check our intention."

Even Food Has Modes

Krishna's next revelation was unexpected—but deeply relatable.

"Even the food people prefer is shaped by the three modes," He said.

"Those in goodness prefer clean, fresh, juicy, wholesome food that increases health and happiness."

"Those in passion go for overly spicy, sour, salty, or bitter foods that may excite the tongue but bring disease and restlessness."

"And those in ignorance eat stale, spoiled, tasteless food—even leftovers from others—unfit for offering to God."

Our food is our fuel—and it shapes our consciousness. Choosing fresh, sattvic food offered to Krishna not only nourishes the body but uplifts the soul.

Sacrifice and the Why Behind It

"Now hear of sacrifice," Krishna said. "Not all sacrifice leads to elevation."

"Sacrifice performed out of duty, with no selfish motive and as directed by scripture, is in goodness."

"When it is done for prestige, recognition, or reward, it is in passion."

"And sacrifice without faith, without purity, without distribution of prasadam, and without proper chanting—is done in ignorance. It yields no true benefit."

Even a small act—if done in devotion, without pride or agenda—has more value than grand shows of charity done for Instagram likes or social praise.

Austerity: Body, Speech, and Mind

Krishna lovingly shared the three kinds of tapasya (austerity):

1. Austerity of the body – Respecting elders, gurus, and God. Maintaining cleanliness and purity.
2. Austerity of speech – Speaking the truth in a way that is kind, beneficial, and non-hurtful.
3. Austerity of the mind – Cultivating peace, simplicity, silence, self-control, and clarity.

"When all three are practised together with faith in Me, and without desire for material gain," Krishna said, "that is austerity in goodness. But if penance is done for fame, admiration, or out of pride—it is passion. If it causes pain to self or others—it is ignorance."

Self-discipline is sacred when it softens your ego and draws you closer to Krishna—not when it hardens your heart or boosts your pride.

Charity with a Pure Heart

"Charity, too, is of three kinds," Krishna continued.

"Goodness means giving in the right way, at the right time, to the right person—without expecting anything in return. Passion gives with expectation, 'What will I gain from this?' And ignorance gives at the wrong time, to unworthy recipients, or with arrogance or disregard."

True giving purifies the heart only when it's free from ego. Even a small offering made with sincerity is more pleasing to Krishna than a million rupees given for show.

The Sacred Vibration: Om Tat Sat

To tie everything together, Krishna revealed the three sacred syllables—Om, Tat, and Sat—which the spiritual masters have used since ancient times.

- Om: The sound of the Supreme Lord.
- Tat: Meaning "that"—the act is not for me, but for the Lord.
- Sat: The eternal truth, the goal of all spiritual practices.

"These three words purify all acts of sacrifice, charity, and penance when remembered with faith," Krishna said. "But if anything is done without faith in Me, even if it appears spiritual, it is called asat—temporary, hollow, and useless in this life or the next."

Spiritual life without faith and connection to Krishna is like a lamp without flame. The outer rituals may exist—but the inner transformation won't happen.

Arjuna Reflects… and So Can We

Arjuna sat in deep thought. He had once believed that worship was just a ritual, food just a choice, giving just a gesture. But now he saw the truth.

Even the smallest acts of life—what we eat, say, give, or endure—can either bind us tighter to illusion, or pull us closer to Krishna.

It's not the action alone—but the intention, the consciousness, and the faith that defines its value.

Krishna's Loving Conclusion

"My dear Arjuna, whatever you do—whether you sacrifice, give, fast, or speak—do it as an offering unto Me. Do it with faith. Do it with love. Do it with scriptural guidance. And I will accept it. And I will accept you."

Key Lessons for the Modern Seeker

1. Faith follows nature, not just belief.

Our faith reflects our inner wiring—the mode of nature we live in shapes the god we serve, the guru we follow, and even the values we uphold.

Not all spirituality is the same. Some chase power, some chase peace, some chase illusion. Check the vibe behind your vibe. Is your "faith" leading to light—or ego?

2. Don't mistake punishment for purity.

Harsh austerities done without compassion or awareness don't elevate—they degrade.

Self-growth isn't about beating yourself up with extreme habits. It's not "No pain, no gain"—it's "Right pain, right gain." Purify with love, not pride.

3. What you eat shapes how you think.

Even food carries energy. Sattvic (pure) food nourishes clarity and devotion; tamasic (spoiled/stale) food clouds the soul.

Your plate is your prayer. Choose meals that nourish not just your body, but also your mood, mindset, and meditation.

4. Give without a hidden agenda.

Charity given with ego or expectation is just a spiritual transaction—not transformation.

Generosity isn't measured by the size of our donation, but the space in our heart. Give quietly. Give sincerely. Give like no one's watching—even online.

5. Rituals without faith are empty shells.

Even noble acts—sacrifice, charity, austerity—become hollow if done without connection to Krishna.

Spirituality isn't aesthetics or performance. It's intention. A yoga pose, a mantra, a donation—all only shine if done with meaning, not marketing.

Chapter 18

The Journey Home—Renunciation, Realisation, and Returning to Krishna

As the chariot rested on the silent plains of Kurukshetra, the sacred dialogue was nearing its end. Arjuna's eyes reflected both clarity and surrender. Yet one question still lingered in his heart.

He turned to Krishna, his divine friend and guide, and asked, "O Madhusudana, O master of the senses, please tell me the essence of renunciation (sannyasa) and renounced action (tyaga). I feel they are not the same. What is true renunciation according to You?"

Krishna, the Lord of the universe, smiled warmly. Arjuna was asking not for theory but the final map for liberation.

What Does It Mean to Renounce?

Krishna said, "O Arjuna, renunciation and tyaga are indeed different. Sannyasa means giving up actions that are born out of selfish desires. Tyaga, however, means giving up the results of all work. One doesn't stop doing his duties—he simply stops claiming the results or rewards as his own."

Krishna explained that some thinkers declare all actions should be renounced. Others argue that acts like sacrifice, charity, and penance must never be given up.

And Krishna, the perfect guide, clarified: "Sacrifice, charity, and penance purify even great souls. These must be performed—but without attachment or expectation. Perform them as your sacred duty. That, My dear Arjuna, is the highest renunciation."

Not All Giving Up Is Spiritual

Then Krishna exposed the subtle shades of false renunciation:

- If a person gives up duties out of illusion, thinking work is bad—that is renunciation in ignorance.
- If he gives them up out of fear, seeking comfort instead of truth—that is renunciation in passion.
- But when a person does his duty, without attachment, without desire for reward—that is renunciation in goodness.

True renunciation isn't about quitting your job, abandoning family, or sitting silently in a forest. It's about working with detachment, not for ego or profit, but for the pleasure of Krishna. Keep the action. Drop the obsession with the result.

Who Really Acts?

Then Krishna revealed a deep secret: "No one can give up activity completely. But when one gives up the attachments for the results, he is truly renounced."

He taught Arjuna that action isn't as simple as "I did it."

"There are five causes behind every action—the body, the doer, the senses, the effort, and the Supersoul (God)."

If someone thinks "I alone am the doer," ignoring these factors, he is in ignorance.

We might think, "I built this business," or "I saved that project." But did we control our breath? Our heartbeat? Our ideas? Krishna reminds us—we're instruments. The Lord within us empowers all action.

Understanding, Determination, and Happiness—in Three Flavours

Krishna now began listing the threefold divisions in every aspect of life:

- Knowledge in goodness sees one undivided spiritual

reality (the spirit soul, part and parcel of God) in all beings.

- Knowledge in passion sees only variety and separation.
- Knowledge in ignorance sees only the body and misses the soul.

Similarly:

- Action in goodness is done as duty, with no attachment.
- Action in passion is driven by ego, desire, and stress.
- Action in ignorance is careless, harmful, and against dharma.

And then Krishna spoke of happiness: "The happiness that begins like poison and ends like nectar—that is in goodness."

"The happiness that feels like nectar at first but turns to poison—that is in passion."

"And happiness born of laziness, sleep, or delusion—that is ignorance."

That 10-minute scroll on social media? It feels good at first—but drains us later.

That one honest hour of chanting God's names, yoga, or seva? It's hard at first—but fills us with joy. Choose the nectar, even if it comes slow.

Every Soul Has a Divine Duty

Krishna now addressed the varna system, not as a birth-based caste, but as qualities born of modes of nature:

- Brahmanas serve by teaching, guiding, and living in purity.
- Kshatriyas lead with courage, protect, and rule justly.
- Vaishyas create prosperity through trade and agriculture.
- Shudras support with service and labour.

Every soul has a nature and purpose. Krishna reminded Arjuna:

"It is better to do your own duty imperfectly than to do another's perfectly. All work in this world is covered by some fault—like fire is covered by smoke. But by worshipping Me through your natural work, you can attain perfection."

You don't have to quit your job to be spiritual. Be a doctor, artist, teacher, engineer—but offer your work to Krishna. Do it with devotion. Do it with dharma.

The Path to Perfection

Krishna now spoke of the ladder to liberation:

1. Perform your duty with detachment.
2. Purify your mind and senses through self-control and introspection.

3. Let go of pride, lust, anger, and possessiveness.
4. Live in a quiet, humble, regulated way, not chasing pleasures.
5. Meditate on Krishna, and be free from ego and dualities.

And then, one reaches the state of divine consciousness—peaceful, equal to all, free from lamentation or craving.

But Krishna was clear: "Only through bhakti—pure devotion—can you truly know Me, O Arjuna."

"When you serve Me with love, I reveal Myself fully. And My devotee, even while working in this world, reaches My eternal abode."

The Final Instruction: Just Surrender

And now, with all truth laid bare, Krishna whispered His most confidential teaching: "O Arjuna, always think of Me. Become My devotee. Worship Me and offer your heart to Me. You will surely come to Me—I promise."

"Abandon all other duties and just surrender unto Me. I will protect you from all sinful reactions. Do not fear."

You don't need to know Sanskrit. You don't need a perfect past. You need only one thing—a sincere heart that says: Krishna, I am Yours.

Arjuna's Awakening

Krishna then paused, giving Arjuna full freedom.

"This knowledge is complete. Now reflect on it and act as you wish."

Krishna does not impose Himself. He creates awareness and lets the individual choose. The choice, after hearing the entire wisdom, lies with us. And thus, we are held accountable for the choices we make.

Arjuna's eyes were no longer clouded. His voice rang with clarity.

"O Krishna, my illusion is gone. I remember who I am, by Your mercy. I am ready. I will do as You instruct."

Sanjaya's Closing Words

Sanjaya, who had witnessed the whole conversation through divine vision, was overwhelmed.

"O King," he said, "as I remember this sacred dialogue between Krishna and Arjuna, my heart dances in ecstasy."

"Wherever there is Krishna, the master of all mystics, and Arjuna, the empowered devotee, there will always be victory, opulence, morality, and everlasting glory. That is my firm conclusion."

This is not just Arjuna's story. It is your story.

You are the soul, sitting in the chariot of the body.

Krishna is your eternal guide, patiently waiting to direct you.

The reins are in your hands. But when you surrender them to Him, He will lead you—not to fleeting success, but to everlasting freedom, joy, and love.

That is the promise of the *Bhagavad Gita.*

That is the song of the Supreme.

Key Lessons for the Modern Seeker

1. Don't quit life—quit attachment.

True renunciation is not abandoning your responsibilities, but giving up the obsession with results. Keep doing your duty—but let go of the ego and expectations.

You don't need to quit your job, family, or ambitions to be spiritual. Just shift your focus: from "What do I get?" to "How can I serve?" Success flows naturally when your work becomes worship.

2. Be a doer, not the controller.

You are not the sole doer. Every action has five causes—including the divine hand of God within. To think "I did it all" is ignorance.

Celebrate your efforts, but stay humble. We didn't write our heartbeat, generate our talent, or plan our destiny. When we remember that we are simply instruments of grace, ego drops—and gratitude rises.

3. Choose the right kind of happiness.

Some joys begin like poison and end as nectar—this is sattvic (in goodness). Others are instant hits but bring long-term ruin—this is rajasic (in passion).

Scrolling endlessly or binge-watching might feel good now—but leaves you empty. Meditation, reflection, chanting, or serving others may seem slow—but they nourish your soul. Invest in the happiness that lasts.

4. Be authentically you.

Better to follow your own path with flaws than someone else's path with perfection. Dharma is unique for each soul.

You don't have to copy someone else's life blueprint. Whether you're a coder, a creator, or a caregiver—your true success lies in doing it with integrity, devotion, and a sense of service.

5. Surrender is the shortcut.

After all teachings, Krishna gives the ultimate instruction: "Just surrender unto Me. I will protect you. Do not fear."

You don't need to have all the answers. You need trust. Let go of the illusion of control. Let Krishna take the reins of your life. That surrender is not weakness—it's the highest strength.

Epilogue

From the Battlefield to the Heart: Your Journey with the *Gita* Begins Now

Dear Reader,

If you have reached this page, know that you are no longer just a reader—you are a seeker. And like Arjuna on the battlefield of Kurukshetra, you have walked through confusion, self-inquiry, revelation, surrender, and ultimately, spiritual awakening.

This wasn't just a story.

It was your story.

The battlefield wasn't just Kurukshetra—it was the field of your own heart. The questions Arjuna asked were your questions too:

Who am I? What is my duty? Why do I suffer? How do I let go? Where do I find peace?

And the answers Krishna gave to Arjuna, He now gives to you.

You've just received the essence of all the Vedas, wrapped in the divine conversation between the Supreme Lord and His beloved devotee. And what was Krishna's final instruction?

"Abandon all other forms of religion and just surrender unto Me. Just come to My shelter. I will deliver you from all sin. Do not fear." *(Gita 18.66)*

That's it. That's the secret. Krishna doesn't want your perfection.

He wants your connection. He wants your heart.

What Happens Next?

You might be wondering—now that the last chapter has been read, what's the next step?

Without applying what we have heard or learnt, the entire effort would be a waste.

The answer is: Begin to live the *Gita*.

- Don't just admire Krishna—invite Him into your life.
- Don't just remember Arjuna's surrender—practise your own.
- Don't just read about bhakti—start chanting, even just

one round 108 times a day and gradually increase: Hare Krishna Hare Krishna, Krishna Krishna Hare Hare. Hare Ram Hare Ram, Ram Ram Hare Hare.

- Don't just understand the soul—treat yourself and others as souls.

You Are Not Alone

The *Gita's* message is not just ancient. It's alive. And so is Krishna. Right now, He sits within your heart, patiently waiting—not to judge, but to guide.

He never forgets you.

He never gives up on you.

And when you turn to Him—even slightly—He runs toward you, with more love than the universe can hold.

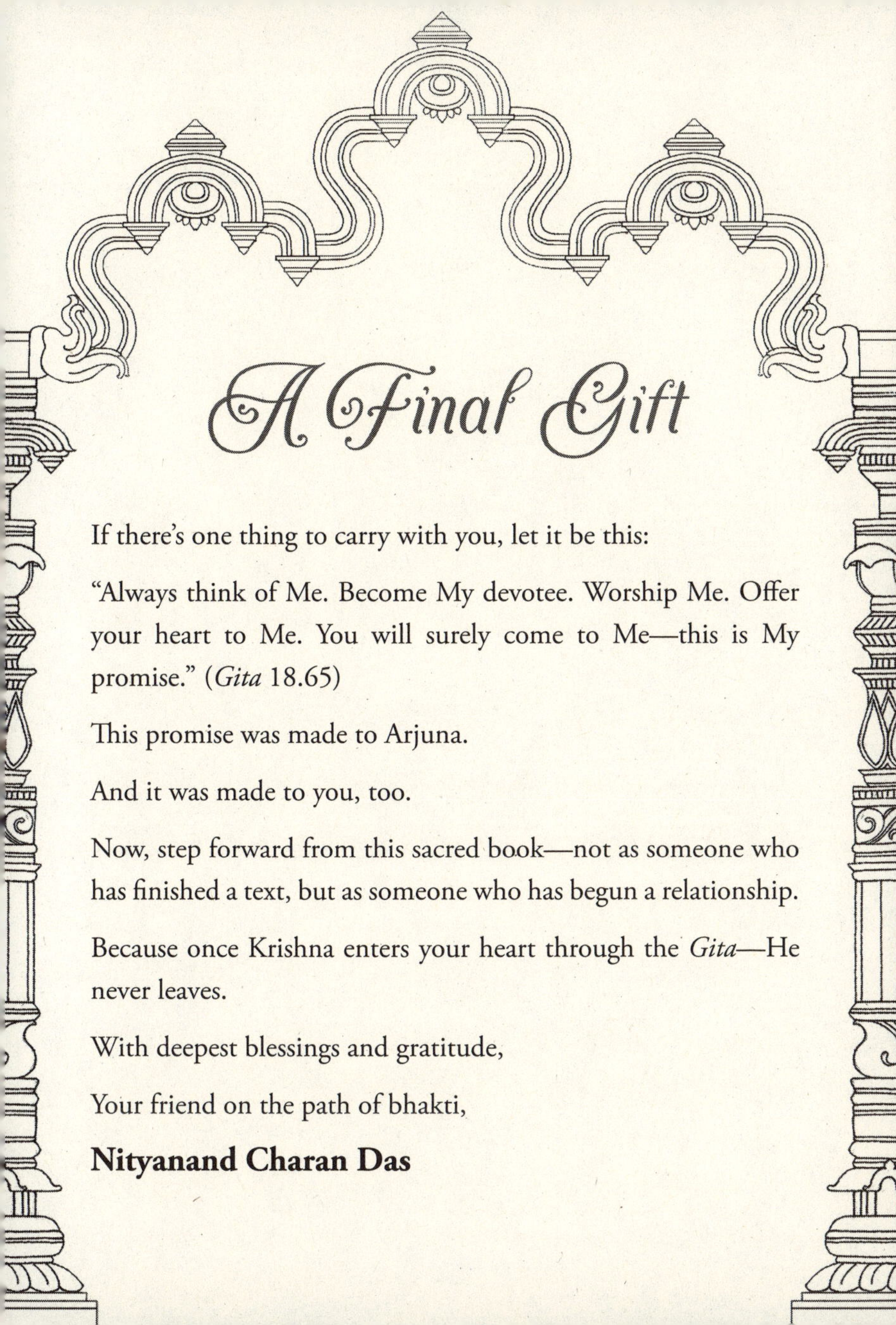

A Final Gift

If there's one thing to carry with you, let it be this:

"Always think of Me. Become My devotee. Worship Me. Offer your heart to Me. You will surely come to Me—this is My promise." (*Gita* 18.65)

This promise was made to Arjuna.

And it was made to you, too.

Now, step forward from this sacred book—not as someone who has finished a text, but as someone who has begun a relationship.

Because once Krishna enters your heart through the *Gita*—He never leaves.

With deepest blessings and gratitude,

Your friend on the path of bhakti,

Nityanand Charan Das

Abouth the Author

Nityanand Charan Das, an esteemed spiritual counsellor and practicing monk for the past 18 years at ISKCON Chowpatty, Mumbai, is a disciple of the world-renowned spiritual leader, philanthropist, and best-selling author, His Holiness Radhanath Swami.

A celebrated author of several national bestsellers, Nityanand Charan Das has captivated readers with works such as A Monk's Almanac, Icons of Grace, and Ask the Monk. His latest book, SHIVA, also has joined the ranks of national bestsellers, offering a profound exploration of the hidden dimensions of Lord Shiva and providing deeper insights into His unexplored persona.

Among his other notable works are Bound by Love, Vedic Tales, and Epic Tales of Wisdom, each reflecting his unique ability to blend timeless wisdom with contemporary relevance.

Deeply committed to enriching urban lives, Nityanand Charan Das aims to help individuals lead lives of purpose, fulfilment, and satisfaction, both professionally and personally. Specializing in mentoring today's youth—children, teenagers, and young professionals—he inspires them to reconnect with their roots and embrace a simpler, happier life.

As a sought-after speaker, he travels extensively worldwide, delivering enlightening discourses on ancient wisdom of the Bhagavad Gita, Shrimad Bhagavatam, Ramayana, and Mahabharata in a manner that resonates with audiences of all ages. His discourses are heard in multiple countries across the globe.

Born into an army family, his early ambition was to join the armed forces. However, through Krishna's divine orchestration, he did not clear the NDA interview despite excelling in his group. This led him to pursue Mechanical Engineering, eventually finding his true calling as a monk at the age of 24.

Over the years, Nityanand Charan Das has served in various capacities, including deity worship, organizing festivals and pilgrimages, and leading vibrant kirtans. Through his outreach, he has nurtured a flourishing spiritual community in Mumbai, across India, and internationally.

His message is simple yet profound:

"Spiritual Life is not a life of Rejection.

It is a life of Connection"

We don't need to give up anything; we only need to embrace this valuable dimension to enrich our lives.